A New Approach to Joyce

Robert S. Ryf

A New Approach to Joyce

THE *Portrait of the Artist* AS A GUIDEBOOK

88

UNIVERSITY OF CALIFORNIA PRESS
Berkeley and Los Angeles
1964

Acknowledgment is made to The Viking Press, Inc. for permission to quote from James Joyce's works: "Chamber Music" from *Collected Poems*, Copyright 1918 by B. W. Huebsch, 1946 by Nora Joyce; *Dubliners; A Portrait of the Artist as a Young Man*, Copyright 1916 by B. W. Huebsch, 1944 by Nora Joyce; and *Finnegans Wake*, Copyright 1939 by James Joyce.

From *Ulysses*, by James Joyce. Copyright 1914, 1918, 1942, 1946 by Norah Joseph Joyce. Reprinted by permission of Random House, Inc.

From *Stephen Hero*, by James Joyce. Copyright 1944 by New Directions. Copyright © 1955 by New Directions. Reprinted by permission of New Directions.

From *Chamber Music, Dubliners,* and *A Portrait of the Artist as a Young Man,* by James Joyce. Reprinted by permission of Jonathan Cape Limited.

From *Stephen Hero, Finnegans Wake,* and *Chamber Music,* by James Joyce. Reprinted by permission of The Society of Authors as the literary representatives of the Estate of the late James Joyce.

From *Ulysses,* by James Joyce. Reprinted by permission of The Bodley Head Ltd.

University of California Press
Berkeley and Los Angeles, California
Cambridge University Press
London, England

Published with the assistance of a grant from the Ford Foundation.

LIBRARY OF CONGRESS CATALOG CARD NUMBER: 61-7522
Manufactured in the United States of America

Acknowledgments

Every Joyce scholar is indebted to his predecessors and teachers. My principal obligation, a considerable one, is to William York Tindall, and I gladly acknowledge it here.

Chapter 9 of this book appeared, in a slightly different form, in *Texas Studies in Literature and Language,* Volume I (Spring, 1959).

R. S. R.

Contents

1

Introduction

This book is intended for the educated reader who is not a Joyce specialist—in other words, for that reader who has been so long and curiously neglected by some Joyce scholars.

There is no doubt that Joyce's writings are complex. As a reader increases his understanding of them—and this is a process requiring diligence and ingenuity—he is tempted to yield to intellectual *hubris* and parade that ingenuity. This, unfortunately, seems to be what much of a certain kind of Joyce scholarship in America amounts to. It consists of web spinning and the manipulation of minute marginalia, written by specialists for specialists, and the nonspecialist who is simply trying to understand Joyce is left out in the cold. Occasionally, the complexity of the criticism seems to surpass that of Joyce. Further, each specialist seems to feel that he and he alone has a corner on Joyce, and is compelled to demolish, or attempt to demolish, all his predecessors. This is a regrettable waste of time and energy.

On the other hand, there are those who, in a laudable attempt to communicate with the reading public have, unfortunately, so oversimplified Joyce as to render him indistinguishable from a dozen or so other modern writers. Very obviously, the trouble with this "common reader" approach is that Joyce is not a common writer.

In this book I shall try to tread, however waveringly,

the middle ground between the two extremes. My aim, quite simply, is to help my readers understand Joyce better by better understanding *A Portrait of the Artist as a Young Man* and its relationship to the other works. I do not claim any corner on Joyce, nor do I seek to demolish any specialists. I hope to illuminate, not to irritate.

None of the above is to suggest, however, that I personally have not been helped in my own understanding of Joyce by the writings of the specialists. I obviously have, and I am indebted to most of them.[1] But what may be useful to me may not necessarily be of help to my readers. In some instances, then, I have filtered and summarized prevalent critical opinions. In other contexts, I have—and I regret I must use this word—translated. Where individual scholars have made significantly original contributions and interpretations, I have of course specifically acknowledged them. On occasion, I even immodestly acknowledge my own.

The entire history of Joyce scholarship has been the gradual revelation of the organic inter-relationship of his works. It is now generally agreed that in theme, imagery, symbolism, and rhythm, his writings are all of one piece. In a sense, he wrote but one book.

We see now, for example, that all Joyce's feminine characters—from the unnamed object of his poems in *Chamber Music,* through Gretta Conroy of "The Dead," Emma Clery of the *Portrait,* and Molly Bloom of *Ulysses,* to Anna Livia Plurabelle of *Finnegans Wake*—in addition to being realized characters in their own right, are also representative aspects of Joyce's archetype of woman. Similarly, the relationship among the central men of his writings—Stephen, Bloom, Earwicker, and the Shem-Shaun polarity now stands revealed as that of the interconnected parts of a whole, the whole in this instance being modern man.

2

This continuity manifests itself in themes as well as characters. Alienation, isolation, the Fall, the search for the father, exile—all these and others function as leitmotivs, to recur again and again in this interwoven body of writing, a recurrence best epitomized by the cyclical rhythm of *Finnegans Wake.*

These relationships are clear now, but they were less clear in the past. The poems of *Chamber Music,* for instance, were typically dismissed as being trivial and empty of meaning until William Y. Tindall penetrated their surfaces and revealed the scope and function of the poems in the larger Joycean framework.[2] *Dubliners* was for many years commonly thought to be merely a collection of naturalistic sketches of the decay of Dublin, until scholars indicated the possibility of larger dimensions.[3] And of course *Ulysses* and *Finnegans Wake* continue to be happy hunting grounds for those intent upon tracing relationships of rhythm, symbol, and image from one work to another.

Perhaps even more remarkable are the history and reputation of the *Portrait.* Appearing in print originally in serial form in the British periodical *The Egoist* in 1914–1915, through the good offices of Ezra Pound, the work was either generally ignored, superficially treated, categorically attacked, or dismissed as unimportant. Two years after the last installment, *The Egoist* collected and printed excerpts from representative reviews of the book. The general tone of these reviews was unfavorable, and curious indeed were some of the objections to the novel. One reviewer felt that Joyce, although a clever novelist, would be at his best in a treatise on drains. Another pontificated that no "clean minded" person would allow the book within reach of his family. Joyce was criticized for being offensive, for lacking humor, and for failing to do justice to Ireland.

A small minority, however, found voice. One reviewer commented on its beauty, and the Italian journalist

3

Diego Angeli, in a surprisingly penetrating article, made some extremely perceptive comments about the style and form of the book.

In the next two decades several well-known figures in the literary world commented on the *Portrait*. H. G. Wells granted that its claim to be literature was as good as the claim of the last book of *Gulliver's Travels,* and regarded it as a worthwhile story of education, written with an unfailing sense of reality. But Wells also felt compelled to pass moral judgment. Joyce, like Swift, he pointed out, had a "cloacal obsession" and wanted to bring back into life some of its seamier aspects, things that "modern drainage and modern decorum" had removed from it. He also criticized Joyce for what he regarded as the needless and unpleasant use of "coarse, unfamiliar" words.

Arnold Bennett read the book because Wells insisted. But he was not impressed, and on the whole the book bored him. He found large sections of it dull and confused, and concluded that the author either did not know what he was doing, or had not known how to do it, or maybe both.

In 1928 Wyndham Lewis, in *Time and Western Man,* passed it off as a French-influenced naturalistic work, that of a second-rate Dublin Maupassant. And three years later, Edmund Wilson in *Axel's Castle* referred to it as a "straight work of naturalistic fiction."

This "naturalistic" label seemed to adhere tenaciously to the novel, a label fixed even more securely to the work by the first American scholar of the early 1940's to attract large-scale attention as an authority on Joyce—Harry Levin. In his *James Joyce: A Critical Introduction,* Levin observed that the *Portrait* "fits squarely into the naturalist tradition." Although admitting that there were "germs of symbolism" in the book, he spoke of its "comparative slightness" as contrasted to Joyce's later writings.

Levin's appraisal of the *Portrait* was not to remain long

4

unchallenged. In 1946, Hugh Kenner, in an essay entitled "The *Portrait* in Perspective," opened up the work for the first time and revealed the larger dimensions that had escaped detection for so long. Calling attention to the complexity of the novel, Kenner revealed, through his intensive if partial analysis, additional layers of inherent meaning, and established many correspondences between it and other works of Joyce. He summed up his observations by pointing out that the three major works of Joyce—the *Portrait, Ulysses,* and *Finnegans Wake*—"are all versions of one another: they simply repeat the same action in different modes." Although this seems an oversimplified view of the relationships among these three works, Kenner was pioneering in this area, and his contribution still looms large.[4]

Subsequent scholarship has further illuminated this path. William Y. Tindall, in his *James Joyce: His Way of Interpreting the Modern World,* discusses all the writings simultaneously under various headings, thus implying the fundamental interrelationships. In his introduction to *Chamber Music* he connects the poems to the novel, and in *The Literary Symbol* he demonstrates, by tracing symbols and images, the continuity that links the *Portrait* to Joyce's other writings.

Although the complexity and importance of the *Portrait* are now generally accepted, there is little agreement as to just where it belongs in the Joyce canon. Until now no one has attempted a full-scale study of the novel and its orientation to each of the other works. And that is what this book is all about.

I believe that the *Portrait,* properly understood, occupies a central position in the Joyce canon. It is a nuclear work, and may properly be considered a guidebook to the rest of his writings. If we understand the *Portrait* and its organic relationship to the other writings, we shall come to understand the other writings better, and our total understanding of Joyce will measurably increase.

Of course, not everyone will agree with my opinion of

5

the *Portrait*. Those who take issue may accuse me of contradicting myself. If the entire history of Joyce scholarship has tended toward establishing the fundamental continuity and reflexiveness of his writings, what sets the *Portrait* apart from the others? May not the same things that may be said about the *Portrait* apply with equal logic to *Chamber Music, Dubliners, Ulysses,* or *Finnegans Wake*? May not any work be used to interpret and illuminate any other? If so, why call the *Portrait* a guidebook? Is there anything unique about it?

I believe that there is. First, a careful reading of the earlier works—*Chamber Music, Dubliners,* and *Stephen Hero*—will reveal that with the writing of the *Portrait* Joyce fulfilled the promise of his remarkable story "The Dead," came of age artistically, and attained full creative power. Second, all Joyce's themes are present in the *Portrait,* and his major techniques are present, at least in embryo. Perhaps most convincingly, in the *Portrait* we find the complete formulation of Joyce's artistic method—the esthetic principles upon which all his works are based. Finally, I offer my personal opinion, challengeable though it may be, that the *Portrait* is esthetically the most pleasing and therefore, in a sense, the best-written of his works.

It will be noted that I have not yet mentioned Joyce's play *Exiles*. This work will be short-changed in the present study. I believe Joyce's achievement in this play to have been slight and little more than a weak and overt reiteration of one of his basic themes. Beyond suggesting a possible explanation for the curious ineptness of the play, therefore, I shall not examine it intensively.

With this one exception, the relationship of the *Portrait* to each of the other major works will be considered in some detail.

2

Understanding Joyce: A Background

SYMBOLISM has had a long and interesting history. Medieval concepts of hierarchy and correspondence legitimized it and gave it a frame of reference, seventeenth- and eighteenth-century science shattered it, and the romantics tried to restore it. These are matters that have been dealt with in detail by many scholars.

I am chiefly interested in distinguishing between what I shall arbitrarily call allegorical symbolism on the one hand and romantic symbolism on the other. In Dante's great allegory *The Divine Comedy* the symbols, in most instances, present little difficulty. When, in Canto I of the *Inferno*, Dante is confronted by a leopard, a lion, and a wolf, we can easily understand that these allegorical animals are, in moral terms, to be translated Worldly Pleasure, Ambition, and Avarice; or, in political terms, Florence, the royal house of France, and the Papal See, respectively. These interpretations accord with a common and universal tradition within a unified frame of reference.

When the common tradition begins to crack and disintegrate, however, as has been true in the modern world, there is a shift from allegorical to romantic symbolism, as writers probe the world beyond the senses and the world beyond reason, as they move from exactitude to inexactitude. The things for which a symbol stands be-

7

come more uncertain, more ambiguous as our world becomes more uncertain and ambiguous.

To understand romantic symbolism, then, we must cultivate a different frame of reference and even a different modality of thought. We must learn to suspend our customary either/or approach by which we sort out reality in the visible universe, and substitute for it a both/and modality that carries us into the invisible universe. We must, in short, cultivate what Keats called the negative capability, ". . . that is, when a man is capable of being in uncertainties, mysteries, doubts, without any irritable reaching after facts and reason."

This flexible attitude of mind, interestingly enough, has been sanctioned by twentieth-century psychologists, who call it ambiguity tolerance. We need the negative capability, or ambiguity tolerance, when we approach the problem of meaning in romantic symbolism. We know what Dante's lion means, but what about Melville's whale? What precisely does it stand for? This leviathan has been said to have something to do variously with God, evil, truth, reality, and irrationality, among other things. The point is that this is a both/and, rather than an either/or, situation. To equate this kind of symbol arbitrarily and algebraically is to emasculate it.

Dante's lion seems transparently clear also when we place it beside Blake's tiger of the poem in which it burns so bright. But, you may say, there is no difficulty here. The tiger, obviously, is Satan. We know this because the recurring question in the poem is "Did He who made the Lamb make thee?" And the Lamb, traditionally and obviously, is Christ. Therefore . . . But it is at this point that the simple explanation seems oversimplified. For let us consider some obvious attributes of the tiger. One might be cruelty. What then about the Lamb? Gentleness? Yes, that fits. Or take another tiger quality —power. The Lamb—weakness? True. And can we not see various other attributes, such as evil, cunning, pride, experience, bound up in this versatile beast? And in

8

each instance can we not also see its opposite in the Lamb? Blake tells us in the poem of the tiger's fearful symmetry, but the tiger begins to tell us also of its fearful versatility. It begins to resemble a chameleon. As does the Lamb. In short, this is another both/and situation.

If this sort of speculation seems to lead us down the garden path, it may be that we are on the road not taken in Frost's poem of that title:

> Two roads diverged in a yellow wood,
> And sorry I could not travel both
> And be one traveler, long I stood
> And looked down one as far as I could
> To where it bent in the undergrowth;

In this poem, the speaker is obviously at a crossroads. But what does this crossroads represent? To some, one road may lead to the city, the other to the country. Others may see a choice of careers involved. Still others may label these roads faith and doubt, individualism and collectivism, conformity and nonconformity. But which interpretation is *right*?

The trouble is that this is the wrong sort of question to ask. We approach the symbol incorrectly when we press for specific and exclusive meaning. It simply will not yield to the either/or approach. What we should do and can do, however, is *to ascertain the area of experience within which the symbol operates, or the fundamental relationship it delineates*. This is something we can find out and, reassuringly, it is something that we can usually agree upon.

Now let's take another look at the tiger and the Lamb. Regardless of what meaning we assign to one, we must assign its opposite to the other. And here, "opposite" is the key word. For what emerges from thinking about Blake's poem is that the area of experience he is talking about is the area of opposites, the paradox of polarity. How do we explain opposites—good versus evil, for example—in our world? Blake does not tell us; he simply

9

raises the question very eloquently. But this is the area of experience within which his basic symbols operate. And this area can be determined fairly objectively.

This is not to say that each reader of the poem will not incline to his own specific interpretation of the symbols. This is natural, and there is certainly nothing wrong with it. But first, to appreciate the richness of the symbol we should ascertain the area of experience in which its cluster of related referents operates, and suspend in our minds, in the best Keatsian fashion, the several complementary possibilities or multiple meanings.

The same situation greets us at Frost's crossroads. We have a basic area of human experience here symbolized, and that basic area is choice—not any *specific* choice but the *problem* of choice. Again, we may have a certain interpretation in mind. This is well and good, but first let us find the nucleus before taking our individual peripheral stations.

It should be apparent by now that one guess is not necessarily as good as another in delineating symbolic meaning. If there is a nucleus of meaning in a symbol, or an area of experience within which a symbol seems to operate, this can usually be determined by close attention to the text. In other words, we make assumptions as to possible meanings, and then we check our assumptions to see if they *work*. For within its own frame of reference a work of art is highly logical, and central meanings can usually be validated by tracing them through the work. In other words, although we bring to the text our own experience and we view the text through the filter of that experience, the direction of movement as we interpret should be toward the text and not toward ourselves. This helps us avoid completely subjective and arbitrary assumptions of meaning.

Here is an extreme example of the purely subjective method. In examining a Joyce text, an enthusiastic female graduate student came upon a passage describing a Friday night fish dinner, and firmly announced that this was a reference to the *Divine Comedy*. The instructor, mindful that Joyce makes much use of Dante in his writings, was most interested in this new bit of evidence, and asked the student how she had arrived at her conclusion. Her chain of reasoning had three links. First of all, they were eating fish. The puzzled instructor admitted this, but pointed out that in a predominantly Catholic city like Dublin this was not a very surprising main course for Friday dinner. But, the student persisted, Dante came from Florence. The now completely mystified instructor granted this fact, whereupon the student announced triumphantly, "And fish always reminds me somehow of Florence!"

What of course invalidated this judgment and provided a good laugh for the rest of the class was the "somehow." In reading symbolist literature, we must substitute relevance for "somehow" and deal in connective meanings that are more universal than idiosyncratic.

To recapitulate briefly—a symbol may suggest more than one meaning at the same time, or the meanings may shift with shifting contexts. A state of mind flexible enough to accommodate and suspend variant readings is essential to the understanding of the symbolic process. But even in the face of multiple meanings we can at least usually determine and agree upon the "nucleus" of the symbol—the area of experience within which it operates, or the fundamental relationship it delineates.

I have not yet discussed a question that undoubtedly occurs to many. We can blithely make assumptions about symbolic meaning, and "verify" them by seeing if they "work" in the text. But how do we know that the meanings we assume are those that the writer intended? The answer is that we do not—and we should not care. Regardless of its excesses and occasional absurdities, the New Criticism (and we must find a different name for it soon; it is not new any more) has made a valuable contribution by focusing our attention on the text rather than on the author. What he *intended* is of secondary importance to what he actually *did*. And the skeptical may well pause to consider the elusive nature of "intention" itself. Is an artist ever completely aware or conscious of what he intends and all he intends? Certainly not, if we believe Jung and Freud at all. Only a part of the artist's intention is conscious and, for all we know, the unconscious part of the intention may well match the unconscious selectivity that leads the reader to his assumptions of symbolic meanings. In this area, then, it is perhaps better to be, like the girl in *Finnegans Wake*, "jung and easily freudened," and to rid ourselves of this traditional compulsion to govern our reactions by what we believe to have been the writer's conscious intention. What is of primary importance is the text and what is in it.

This is not to say, however, that writers do not consciously employ symbols and "intend" many if not most of the meanings the alert reader ferrets out. Clearly they do, and this is particularly true with Joyce, who emerges as one of the most "intentive" writers of all time. It is disconcerting to pursue an ingenious journey after supposedly original meaning and emerge on the other side of the symbol only to find Joyce sitting there paring his nails, smirking, and wondering what kept us. As this process is repeated time after time, it arouses an admiration rather than an affection for him. The point is, however, that we are led to an understanding of Joyce's intention by the evidence of the text itself, and that is as it should be.

This rather meandering journey into symbolism has meant to suggest that in symbolist literature, such as that of Joyce, the symbols themselves are primary vehicles of meaning as they amplify and enrich the narrative material. If we do not know how to approach them properly, the total meaning of the work, elusive at best, tends to fly out the window.

Total meaning is, after all, what we are after. To grasp it or sense it, we must realize that all the parts of a symbolist work operate together to produce or, as Joyce would say, radiate it. The narrative element—plot—is only one element of this combination. The nondiscursive formal elements, such as rhythm, image, structure, and symbol reinforce or frequently override the narrative element in conveying total meaning.

In other words, symbolist literature needs to be re-read. With each reading, new awarenesses produce new meanings. But here I must object to the fashionable phrase, "levels of meaning," so often applied to symbolist literature. This is misleading. As someone has pointed out, a work of art is all surface. Or, to put it another way, the work of literature is *all* there, *all* the time. There are no levels of meaning as such. There are, rather, levels of awareness on the part of the reader.

3

The "Portrait" Itself

ON THE NARRATIVE LEVEL, the *Portrait* presents the formative years of the young, proud, and frequently arrogant intellectual and esthete Stephen Dedalus. The work
is essentially the story of a developing artistic consciousness from earliest childhood recollections to the moment
of self-imposed exile when the twenty-year-old Stephen
invokes his mythical namesake and leaves for Paris and
what he hopes will be a life of artistic freedom and creativity.

We are presented at the outset with a series of undifferentiated infantile responses to environment:

> Once upon a time and a very good time it was
> there was a moocow coming down along the road
> and this moocow that was down along the road met
> a nicens little boy named baby tuckoo. . . .
>
> His father told him that story: his father looked
> at him through a glass: he had a hairy face.
>
> He was baby tuckoo, the moocow came down the
> road where Betty Byrne lived: she sold lemon
> platt. . . .
>
> When you wet the bed, first it is warm then it
> gets cold. His mother put on the oilsheet. That had
> the queer smell.

All five senses are represented here: the sight of the
moocow and the father's hairy face, the sound of the
story, the taste of the lemon platt (a kind of candy),

the smell of the oilsheet, and the feel of wetness. The child Stephen responds first to his father, then to his mother, and then to aunt, great-uncle, and neighbors as his horizon expands.

Segments of experience on the playground and in school follow as Stephen, and with him the reader, differentiates his environments. We can see already an "apartness" about him. Physically he is small and weak, unable to take part in the boisterous games enjoyed by his schoolmates. Intellectually he makes an attempt at self-orientation uncommon for his age by writing an inscription in his geography book:

> *Stephen Dedalus*
> *Class of Elements*
> *Clongowes Wood College*
> *Sallins*
> *County Kildare*
> *Ireland*
> *Europe*
> *The World*
> *The Universe*

His moods at Clongowes Wood alternate between apprehension and loneliness, and he becomes ill. Thoughts of death and dreams of the sea and of the dead Parnell flit through the mind of the feverish nine-year-old boy.

The scene now changes to the Christmas dinner at home. The table becomes a battleground as a bitter dispute over Parnell breaks out, with Stephen's aunt Dante stanchly defending priests, Stephen's father and Mr. Casey castigating them in their angry defense of Parnell, and Stephen's mother and great-uncle Charles trying vainly to conciliate the disputants. At the climax of the rancorous quarrel, Dante stalks fiercely to the door:

> At the door Dante turned round violently and shouted down the room, her cheeks flushed and quivering with rage:
>
> —Devil out of hell! We won! We crushed him to death! Fiend!

The door slammed behind her.

Mr. Casey, freeing his arms from his holders, suddenly bowed his head on his arms with a sob of pain.

—Poor Parnell! he cried loudly. My dead king!

He sobbed loudly and bitterly.

Stephen, raising his terrorstricken face, saw that his father's eyes were full of tears.

Back at school, Stephen is directly introduced to ideas of authority and punishment. Having broken his glasses, he is unjustly "pandied" (beaten with a cane or pandybat) as a "lazy little schemer" by one of the Jesuit priests, Father Dolan. Egged on by the other boys, Stephen reports the injustice to the rector of the school, and is hailed as a minor hero by his schoolmates.

Chapter II brings the boy closer to adolescence. Kept at home because of his father's financial difficulties, of which the boy is only dimly aware, Stephen divides his time among walking, playing, and reading. His peregrinations, variously with his great-uncle, father, and a youthful gang, serve to acquaint him with Dublin and its environs. His reading, interestingly enough, centers on the story of an exile: *The Count of Monte Cristo*. His own rootlessness is symbolized and accentuated by the moving van at the door, as his father's financial situation worsens.

A young and proud intellectualism emerges: "The noise of children at play annoyed him and their silly voices made him feel, even more keenly than he had felt at Clongowes, that he was different from others. He did not want to play. He wanted to meet in the real world the unsubstantial image which his soul so constantly beheld." He begins to "taste the joy of his loneliness" and privately tries his hand at writing poetry, which he then hides.

Stephen now returns to school, this time to Belvedere College. Here his isolation is emphasized by brushes with authority in the classroom and by his refusal to

16

conform outside the class. This refusal subjects him to the ridicule and abuse of his classmates, who are infuriated by his unwillingness to concede that Tennyson is a better poet than Byron.

Stephen becomes increasingly aware of his failure to establish communication with his father and the other members of his family, and of the ever-widening gulf between him and them. The "wasting fires of lust" overwhelm him, and he seeks "to appease the fierce longings of his heart before which everything else was idle and alien." Caring little that his is a life which has grown to be a tissue of lies and is drifting into mortal sin, he feels that nothing is sacred to the "savage desire within him to realize the enormities which he brooded on." He prowls the city at night, and inevitably finds his way to the brothel quarter.

In Chapter III we witness an abrupt stopping of Stephen's debauch. At a religious retreat Father Arnall, Stephen's aged teacher from Clongowes Wood, preaches a terrifying sermon on the horrors of hell and eternal damnation. Stephen is overwhelmed with the realization of his sins: "Every word of it was for him. Against his sin, foul and secret, the whole wrath of God was aimed. The preacher's knife had probed deeply into his disclosed conscience and he felt now that his soul was festering in sin."

As Stephen contemplates his lusts ("Mad! Mad! Was it possible he had done these things?"), he is overcome with feelings of shame and unworthiness. But shame changes to stark horror as the preacher describes hell in detail:

Consider then what must be the foulness of the air of hell. Imagine some foul and putrid corpse that has lain rotting and decomposing in the grave, a jellylike mass of liquid corruption. Imagine such a corpse a prey to flames, devoured by the fire of burning brimstone and giving off dense choking fumes of nauseous loathsome decomposition. And then imagine this sickening stench, multiplied a millionfold and a millionfold again from the millions upon millions of fetid carcasses massed together in the reeking darkness, a huge and rotting human fungus.

The stench of hell is not the only particular that the unrelenting preacher delves into. He vividly sketches other physical torments: pains of fire, of the company of the damned, and of the presence of devils. But these are as nothing compared to the spiritual pains of loss of grace, of conscience, of extension, intensity, and eternity.

Stephen carries an intolerable burden of shame, guilt, and terror back to his room. But no sanctuary awaits him there. Instead, a vision of hell opens before his eyes:

> . . . stinking, bestial, malignant, a hell of lecherous goatish fiends. For him! For him!
>
> He sprang from the bed, the reeking odour pouring down his throat, clogging and revolting his entrails. Air! The air of heaven! He stumbled towards the window, groaning and almost fainting with sickness. At the washstand a convulsion seized him within; and, clasping his cold forehead wildly, he vomited profusely in agony.

This spasm of nausea, literal and symbolic catharsis, affords a degree of relief. He prays earnestly for forgiveness, musters firm purpose of amendment, seeks out a chapel and pours out his clogged confession. The next morning he receives communion.

In Chapter IV we see a devout Stephen making a determined effort at a life of mortification, chastity, and devotion. The director of the college summons him for an interview about his vocation. Inquiring whether Stephen has ever felt a call, the director directs the youth's attention to the Jesuit order. The boy leaves, pondering the possibility of the Reverend Stephen Dedalus, S.J. But he rejects the idea, realizing that he would "never swing the thurible before the tabernacle as priest." He realizes that his destiny lies apart from any religious or social order, that he must acquire his own wisdom. To do this he must not retreat from the world but participate in it, pitfalls and all: "The snares of the world were its ways of sin. He would fall. He had not yet fallen but he would fall silently, in an instant. Not to fall was too hard, too hard: and he felt the silent lapse of his soul, as it would be at some instant to come, falling, falling, but not yet fallen, still unfallen, but about to fall."

With these accompanying overtones of suspended Lucifer and Icarus, Stephen symbolizes his final decision:

> He crossed the bridge over the stream of the Tolka, and turned his eyes coldly for an instant toward the faded blue shrine of the blessed Virgin which stood fowlwise on a pole in the middle of a hamshaped encampment of poor cottages, then, heading to the left, he followed the lane which led up to his house. The faint sour stink of rotted cabbages came towards him from the kitchen gardens on the rising ground above the river. He smiled to think that it was this disorder, the misrule and confusion of his father's house and the stagnation of vegetable life, which was to win the day in his soul.

Stephen now wanders by the seashore, in prelude to what is probably the climactic incident in the novel. The spells of sea, sky, and language work on him. The greeting cries of youthful swimmers, acquaintances of his, build with a kind of contrapuntal rhythm to a vision evoked by the calling of his name:

> Now, at the name of the fabulous artificer, he seemed to hear the noise of dim waves and to see a winged form flying above the waves and slowly climbing the air. What did it mean? Was it a quaint device opening a page of some medieval book of prophecies and symbols, a hawklike man

flying sunward above the sea, a prophecy of the end he had been born to serve and had been following through the mists of childhood and boyhood, a symbol of the artist forging anew in his workshop out of the sluggish matter of the earth a new soaring imperishable being?

His heart trembles at the apparition, and his throat aches to utter hawklike sounds to the wind. This is his call to his true vocation, not of priest but of artificer, of artist. Yes, he affirms triumphantly, he will create imperishable living beauty out of his soul. He wades in the sea, alone, happy, contemplating this adumbration of his function and destiny.

Now he sees a girl standing in the water, alone, gazing out to sea. "She seemed like one whom magic had changed into the likeness of a strange and beautiful sea-bird." She returns his gaze quietly, without shame, and in that instant Stephen undergoes a kind of conversion, but again the realm is secular. He is reborn to earthly, mortal beauty. His soul cries out with "profane joy," and he plunges across the strand in ecstasy, singing wildly to the sea, greeting the life that has called to him: "Her image had passed into his soul for ever and no word had broken the holy silence of his ecstasy. Her eyes had called him and his soul had leaped at the call. To live, to err, to fall, to triumph, to recreate life out of life!"

Stephen wanders on, unmindful of time and place. Finally he wearily stretches out on the sand and experiences his ultimate, Dantesque vision:

He closed his eyes in the languor of sleep. His eyelids trembled as if they felt the vast cyclic movement of the earth and her watchers, trembled as if they felt the strange light of some new world. His soul was swooning into some new world, fantastic, dim, uncertain as under sea, traversed by cloudy shapes and beings. A world, a glimmer, or a flower? Glimmering and trembling, trembling and unfolding, a breaking light, an opening flower, it spread in endless succession to itself, breaking in full crimson and unfolding and fading to palest rose, leaf by leaf and wave of light by wave of light, flooding all the heavens with its soft flushes, every flush deeper than other.

This vision, probably the highest point of the novel, is perhaps Stephen's closest approach to communion in any sense of the word. It is a condition not approximated until, years and pages later, near the end of *Ulysses,* Stephen sees the light in Molly's window. Here surely, the earlier scene enriches the later, which without this borrowing and transference of rich reinforcement would be greatly impoverished.

Chapter V brings us abruptly back to the sordid realities of watery tea, crusts of fried bread, and pawn tickets. At the university Stephen discourses briefly on esthetics to the dean, borrowing from Aristotle and Aquinas and setting the stage for his later expansion of the subject. We are afforded brief glimpses of certain of his contemporaries: Cranly, MacCann, Davin, Moynihan, Temple, and Lynch. We also receive hints of Emma Clery, a more shadowy figure in the *Portrait* than in *Stephen Hero.*

Stephen's isolation increases. He refuses to sign a petition for universal peace, and is criticized by the group. Davin probes Stephen's condition, calling him a "terrible" man who is "always alone." "A born sneerer," in his heart he is still an Irishman but his "pride is too powerful." But Stephen dissociates himself from his environment with what is one of the key statements of the *Portrait:* "—When the soul of a man is born in this country there are nets flung at it to hold it back from flight. You talk to me of nationality, language, religion. I shall try to fly by those nets." Amid Lynch's mundane interruptions, Stephen now goes on to discuss esthetic theory. As I shall attempt to show in a later chapter, these theories explain the structure of Joyce's works. I merely summarize the theories here.

The tragic emotion or the dramatic emotion, he says, is static. The feelings of desire and loathing excited by improper art are kinetic. But in the proper esthetic emotion, which is static, the mind is arrested and raised above desire and loathing. This stasis is called forth, prolonged, and at last dissolved by what he calls the "rhythm of beauty": in an esthetic whole, the relation of part to part, part to whole, or whole to part.

To speak of these things, to try to understand them, and to try constantly and humbly to express them—this, according to Stephen, is art. Art, then, is the human disposition of sensible or intelligible matter for an esthetic and. This esthetic end will be served if the matter is arranged satisfyingly. Beauty will be achieved. Stephen here adapts Aquinas to his purpose: "Aquinas says: *Ad pulcritudinem tria requiruntur integritas, consonantia, claritas.* I translate it so: *Three things are needed for beauty, wholeness, harmony and radiance.*" These qualities correspond to the phases of apprehension of the esthetic object. First, the mind draws a boundary line about the object to be apprehended, separating it from its immeasurable background of space and time. It is apprehended as one thing, one whole. This is *integritas.*

Second, the apprehender passes from point to point of the esthetic object, perceiving the relationship of part to part balanced within its limits, and thus experiences the rhythm of its structure. The synthesis of immediate perception is followed by the analysis of apprehension: ". . . You apprehend it as complex, multiple, divisible, separable, made up of its parts, the result of its parts and their sum, harmonious. That is *consonantia.* . . ."

Finally, the object is perceived to be the thing that it is and no other thing. This synthesis, the only logically and esthetically permissible one now, reveals the radiance, the scholastic *quidditas* or whatness of the thing. The contemplative instant at which it is apprehended by the mind, which has been arrested by its wholeness and fascinated by its harmony, is the luminous silent stasis of esthetic pleasure.

Stephen now differentiates what he calls the three forms of art: the lyrical, in which the artist presents his image in immediate relation to himself; the epical, wherein he presents his image in mediate relation to himself and others; the dramatic, in which he presents his image in immediate relation to others. The lyrical form, he says, is the simplest verbal vesture of an instant of emotion, a kind of rhythmic cry, in which the utterer is more conscious of the emotion than of himself as experiencing the emotion. From this form emerges the epical form in which the center of emotional gravity is equidistant from the artist himself and from others. Here the personality of the artist has passed into the narration, and flows around the persons and the action, surrounding them like a vital sea. And finally:

The dramatic form is reached when the vitality which has flowed and eddied round each person fills every person with such vital force that he or she assumes a proper and intangible esthetic life. The personality of the artist, at first a cry or a cadence or a mood and then a fluid and lambent narrative, finally refines itself out of existence, impersonalizes itself, so to speak. . . . The artist, like the God of the creation, remains within or behind or above his handiwork, invisible, refined out of existence, indifferent, paring his fingernails.

In the next section of this final chapter there is an abrupt change from the expository to the lyrical, a mood or condition strongly reminiscent of *Chamber Music*. Stephen awakes near dawn. ("His soul was all dewy wet.") Tentative lines for a villanelle form in his mind, and he scribbles them on an empty cigarette packet. Alternating between composition and meditation on

23

the girl who is the object of the poem, he relives his relationship with her: moments of anger, moments of envy and wounded pride, the moment of fruition. We see the raw materials of the poem transformed and transmuted in the mind of the maker, and fruition involves not only woman but poem. The villanelle is complete:

> Are you not weary of ardent ways,
> Lure of the fallen seraphim?
> Tell no more of enchanted days.
>
> Your eyes have set man's heart ablaze
> And you have had your will of him.
> Are you not weary of ardent ways?
>
> Above the flame the smoke of praise
> Goes up from ocean rim to rim.
> Tell no more of enchanted days.
>
> Our broken cries and mournful lays
> Rise in one eucharistic hymn.
> Are you not weary of ardent ways?
>
> While sacrificing hands upraise
> The chalice flowing to the brim,
> Tell no more of enchanted days.
>
> And still you hold our longing gaze
> With languorous look and lavish limb!
> Are you not weary of ardent ways?
> Tell no more of enchanted days.

This technically perfect villanelle—with its images of fallen seraphim suggesting both Lucifer and Icarus, broken cries, eucharist, chalice, and lavish limbs—effectively recapitulates Stephen's condition.

He now passes into his pre-flight period. Standing significantly enough on the steps of the library, he watches birds on a late March evening. Obvious symbols of departure, they seem to him auguries, but whether for good or evil he does not know. Aware of vocation, he is not yet aware of destination. His fabulous antecedents Dædalus and Hermes Trismegistus crowd in upon him, and move him to fear and uneasiness at the uncertainty that lies ahead. But as the birds wheel overhead once more, affirming his imminent departure, he experiences a "soft liquid joy" and feels in his heart "the soft peace of silent spaces of fading tenuous sky above the waters, of oceanic silence, of swallows flying through the seadusk over the flowing waters."

Later, he sees Emma Clery and makes his final renunciation of her: "Well then let her go and be damned to her! She could love some clean athlete who washed himself every morning to the waist and had black hair on his chest. Let her."

He walks with Cranly and reveals not only his dispute with his mother but also how the dispute bears upon his creed. She has asked him to make his Easter duty, and he has refused:

—Why not?—Cranly said.

—I will not serve—answered Stephen.

—That remark was made before—Cranly said calmly.

—It is made behind now—said Stephen hotly.

Rejecting Cranly's ideas of religion and mother love, Stephen reveals his own agnosticism, announces his imminent departure, and expands his credo: "I will not serve that in which I no longer believe, whether it call itself my home, my fatherland or my church: and I will try to express myself in some mode of life or art as freely as I can and as wholly as I can, using for my defence the only arms I allow myself to use, silence, exile and cunning."

The final section of the novel, in the form of diary entries, reveals Stephen as, figuratively, he puts his affairs in order for his flight. A last look at the girl, at Cranly, Davin, home, and school, gives way to the irresistible urge to be off. ("Away! Away! The spell of arms and voices. . . .") And finally:

> April 26. Mother is putting my new secondhand clothes in order. She prays now, she says, that I may learn in my own life and away from home and friends what the heart is and what it feels. Amen. So be it. Welcome, O life! I go to encounter for the millionth time the reality of experience and to forge in the smithy of my soul the uncreated conscience of my race.

> April 27. Old father, old artificer, stand me now and ever in good stead.

Thus invoking the fabulous artificer, claiming him as father, Stephen proclaims his final release from the nets that have held him. The fledgling has left the nest. The exile has flown.

The foregoing summary of the *Portrait* is, of course, merely the bare skeleton of the novel. No paraphrase, however lengthy, can reproduce the book. Around this bare skeleton of narrative are grouped images, rhythms, symbols, and changes of tone which not only reinforce meanings but often determine and carry them. Certain aspects of the *Portrait*, then, are nondiscursive, and invite contemplation while evading explication. Nevertheless, this summary should serve to indicate the general action of the narrative, and should also serve as a basis for considering certain of the central themes of the novel.

First, we may safely postulate isolation or alienation as one of these central themes, if not the principal one. Stephen's is the epitome of the isolation experienced by the creative nonconformist intellectual and esthete. In rebellion against his environment, he turns successively for refuge to home, Church, love, and successively finds none in any of these potential sanctuaries.

Stephen is set apart by name, physique, and creed. As a young boy he is small and weak, unable to participate in the games of his contemporaries. His name is singled out early. "What kind of a name is that?" asks a playmate. Later, another calls it a queer name. As we shall see, this motif is reintroduced in *Ulysses*. Probably Joyce had an additional purpose in singling out Stephen's name for comment, as will be discussed in Chapter 10.

One aspect of Stephen's isolation has to do with his relationship to authority and his rebellion against it. At the outset we are presented with a dominant image pattern. A childish resolution to marry a neighbor girl meets with his mother's suggestion that an apology is necessary and his Aunt Dante's comment with its accompanying rhyme:

—O, if not, the eagles will come and pull out his eyes.—

> Pull out his eyes,
> Apologise,
> Apologise,
> Pull out his eyes.

This punishment motif recurs in the scene in which Stephen is unjustly pandied, and again more strongly in the small-scale inquisition that follows a discussion between Stephen and some of his schoolmates about the relative merits of the poets Tennyson and Byron. The conformists damn Byron as a heretic. Stephen retorts his indifference to this charge and affirms Byron's superiority. The shocked and enraged boys attack him and force him back against a barbed wire fence:

—Admit that Byron was no good.
—No.
—Admit.
—No.
—Admit.
—No. No.

At last after a fury of plunges he wrenched himself free. His tormentors set off toward Jones's Road, laughing and jeering at him, while he, half blinded with tears, stumbled on, clenching his fists madly and sobbing.

This motif of rebellion against conformity and authority reappears in later sections of the novel. Stephen, having already rejected the solicitations of the Jesuits, rejects Davin's, or conformity's, notions of nationality and Cranly's, or conformity's, ideas of religion and mother love.

Stephen's isolation is patently self-induced. He would not be set apart if he would conform, but he will not conform. Increasingly conscious of the esthetic and intellectual gulf between him and his environment, he learns to cherish his solitude. His isolation coalesces into doctrine—that of the three nets—then hardens into creed. ("I will not serve that in which I no longer believe.")

This alienation is not confined to nationality and religion; it is also manifested in family relationships. The Christmas quarrel over the dead Parnell is an early estranging incident to the young boy. He grows steadily apart from his father, and realizes that the two of them are separated by "an abyss of fortune or temperament." He contemplates his relationship to the rest of his family: "He saw clearly, too, his own futile isolation. He had not gone one step nearer the lives he had sought to approach nor bridged the restless shame and rancour that had divided him from mother and brother and sister."

The final break with his mother occurs when he refuses to perform his Easter duty. In *Ulysses* we learn that this conflict has continued to the day of her death: summoned home from Paris, Stephen refuses her dying request to kneel and pray for her. He still will not serve.

It may be that in Stephen's mind, thoughts of mother, country, and religion are inextricably interconnected. Having rejected one, he must reject the others. Certainly the maternal images Joyce uses through the novel —cow, milk—may function in all three categories. The moocow on the road in the child's story that opens the *Portrait* reappears in various contexts as Stephen is at first drawn to the cow with its various attendants, then repelled by it. As we shall see later, this particular image reappears functionally in *Ulysses.* In a sense, the entire *Portrait* is an expansion of the story of the moocow. Stephen listens to it, then rejects it.

In addition to mother, country, and religion, Stephen also rejects—perhaps most significantly—his father. His final glib enumeration to Cranly of his father's attributes and minor accomplishments is instructive: "A medical student, an oarsman, a tenor, an amateur actor, a shouting politician, a small landlord, a small investor, a drinker, a good fellow, a storyteller, somebody's secretary, something in a distillery, a taxgatherer, a bankrupt and at present a praiser of his own past." This externalized description comments most directly upon the completeness of Stephen's break with his father.

But this rejection of the nominal father creates a vacuum that Stephen's nature abhors. Thus another central theme is here postulated: the search for a father. This motif, which is developed throughout *Ulysses,* is in the *Portrait* merely introduced. We see Stephen in his first try at the role of Telemachus, as he grabs at a skyhook by hopefully invoking his mythical namesake. But it does not work, and the young exile is soon to learn that mythical wings are not strong enough for sustained flight.

These, then, seem to be the central themes of the *Portrait:* rejection, alienation, isolation, exile, the Fall, the search for the father. These ideas are postulated, reiterated, and reinforced throughout the novel by discourse, dialogue, and connected imagery. But Joyce uses yet another device, one to which far too little attention has been paid. I refer to the rhythmic patterns that constitute the basic structure of the novel and that reinforce its themes.

Structure implies parts or subdivisions, and the most

obvious subdivisions are the chapters. Or we may sub-divide in a different manner by regarding the novel as a succession of climaxes of rejection in the various categories of family, Church, and country. But a careful reading of the *Portrait* will reveal another system of organization that is more essential to Joyce's purpose—sometimes coinciding with chapter divisions and sub-divisions, sometimes not. This system of organization has to do with rhythm, which, as we have seen, Joyce defines as the relationship of part to part; more par-ticularly, it involves changes of rhythm. Stephen, at one point in the story, hears the conversation of some students: "Their voices reached his ears as if from a distance in interrupted pulsation." The phrase "inter-rupted pulsation" is a useful description of the tech-nique Joyce used to reinforce, rhythmically and thus structurally, his central themes.

The interrupted pulsations embodied in the *Portrait* are of several kinds. Some serve as transitions, others as points of arrest; some create contrasts that highlight what is before or after; some others create a con-trapuntal pattern; and still others, patterns of tension-relaxation or inflation-deflation. This last-mentioned pattern will be considered in detail in Chapter 10.

Many of these changes of rhythm are easily identi-fiable. For example, his aunt Dante's little rhyme ("Pull out his eyes,/Apologise"), which initiates the punish-ment theme at the very beginning of the novel, is fol-lowed by an abrupt change of scene to a playground swarming with boys, thus bringing us to a point of arrest or fixation. Tension is followed by relaxation (not resolu-tion, for in Joyce tensions are seldom resolved, unless we interpret the entire work as resolution), and the contrast between what is before and what is after serves in this instance to prolong and heighten the image of what is before.

The very young Stephen contemplates wild roses and wonders if somewhere in the world there might be

30

a green rose instead of a red one. This excursion into artistic imagination is abruptly terminated as the school bell rings and the students file out of the classrooms. The sudden contrast here emphasizes the gulf between the ideal and the real, or the inner and outer reality, which is certainly a fundamental aspect of Stephen's isolation.

Later, Stephen in bed recalls a line from a prayer: "Visit, we beseech Thee, O Lord, this habitation and drive away from it all. . . ." At this precise point in the prayer, thoughts of home and holiday abruptly intrude. Here we get a curious effect. "Habitation" naturally signifies home, and induces thoughts of it; significantly, however, the juxtaposition occurs before the rest of the sentence, "the snares of the enemy," is reached in the prayer. Thus the fragment of the prayer, because of this sudden arrest, now suggests punishment rather than protection, rejection rather than refuge —another reinforcement of the idea of alienation from home which is basic to the *Portrait*.

Before he goes home to the ill-fated Christmas dinner, Stephen dreams of the dead Parnell and his aunt Dante walking silently and proudly past the mourners. Then, abruptly, he is home at Christmas. As a result of this pulsation, the image of aunt Dante versus the mourners persists and effectively sets the stage for the controversy to come. And at the end of the episode, the image of Stephen's terror-stricken face is superimposed by contrast upon the following scene in which schoolboys stand in little groups, talking together. Thus Stephen's apartness is reiterated.

The gulf between the inner life and the outer is nowhere more emphasized than by the change of rhythm in the section in which Stephen realizes his isolation and wishes so desperately "to meet in the real world the unsubstantial image which his soul so constantly beheld." In that projected meeting, "he would be transfigured, weakness and timidity and inexperience would fall from him in the magic moment." But with the following jarring juxtaposition the world of external reality intrudes abruptly: "Two great yellow caravans had halted one morning before the door and men had come tramping into the house to dismantle it."

About halfway through the novel these interrupted pulsations begin to form themselves into contrapuntal patterns. The first of these is in the section describing Stephen's reactions to the sermons at the religious retreat:

> Flames burst forth from his skull like a corolla, shrieking like voices:
> —Hell! Hell! Hell! Hell! Hell!—
> Voices spoke near him:
> —On hell.—
> —I suppose he rubbed it into you well.—
> —You bet he did. He put us all into a blue funk.—
> —That's what you fellows want: and plenty of it to make you work.—

These interjections and subsequent ones about the weather serve to point up the contrast between Stephen's terror and the complacency of the others, between his own Hell with a capital "H" and others', lower-case, hell, thus highlighting and isolating his own reactions.

Counterpoint is used again in the climactic episode —the scene at the beach. Stephen eyes the drifting clouds, hears a confused music within, and is aware of his imagination calling to him out of the silence:

> Again! Again! Again! a voice from beyond the world was calling.
> —Hello, Stephanos!—
> —Here comes The Dedalus!—
> —Ao! . . . Eh, give it over, Dwyer, I'm telling you or I'll give you a stuff in the killer for yourself. . . . Ao!—

This interweaving of inner summons and outer banter which continues for a substantial part of the scene effectively epitomizes the clash between inner and outer realities which contributes heavily to Stephen's isolation.

Similarly, in his prolonged discourse on esthetics, the interweaving of his profundities with Lynch's irrelevant and irreverent interruptions and observations creates a rhythmic pattern that embodies strong suggestions of the gulf between Stephen and his contemporaries. Images of cow dung, Venus' backside, and a drunken evening intrude on Aquinas, or Stephen's version of Aquinas, and function by disruption as effective agents of alienation.

This analysis of Joyce's use of rhythm is by no means exhaustive. There are many more such changes of rhythm throughout the novel. But we are interested here in simply understanding the technique whereby Joyce, both as a skilled contrapuntist and as a juxtaposer of incongruities, reinforces his themes structurally. In addition to this rhythm of structure, he also employs what might be called the rhythm of image, a device that functions in much the same manner as his structural rhythms.

On the first page of the novel we are introduced to three streams of connected imagery that recur in various later sections: imagery of red and green, hot and cold, wet and dry. The first chapter is liberally sprinkled with these polarities. They form a complicated pattern, and it is difficult to assign consistent meanings to them. At the outset, wetness is considered first in connection with warmth, then with cold: "When you wet the bed, first it is warm then it gets cold." Here the wet warmth seems regressively attractive and the subsequent wet cold repulsive to the infant Stephen. Later, cold wetness is identified with the "square ditch" or latrine at the school, and becomes to the boy an epitomizing image of the undesirable. Warmth in general is attractive, but Stephen's pre-Christmas fever is not, nor are the flames of hell, which are so graphically depicted in the sermon

33

at the retreat. Coldness is in general repulsive, particularly when combined with wetness; yet it is by the cold wet sea, which Stephen fears, that the apparition of his fabulous hawklike ancestor is manifested to him. He then wades in the sea and, perhaps because of this venturesome dislocation of the attraction-repulsion polarity, is granted the sight of the girl and his later vision of the rose. It should be noted, however, that this vision is revealed to him when he is on dry land. The hot-cold and wet-dry polarities seem inextricably interwoven, then, and it may only be indicated that in general warmth-wetness implies security for the boy (the attendant regressive overtones are obvious here) and that cold-wetness implies rejection. But the dislocations of these polarities suggest the dislocations of Stephen's life, the rejections that inexorably follow his attempts to find refuge and sanctuary, and his final realization of his inevitable exile.

Similarly, the red-green relationship seems ambiguous. As a small child, Stephen transmutes the conventional color of roses in a song:

O, the wild rose blossoms
On the little green place.
He sang that song. That was his song.
O, the green wothe botheth.

When as a schoolboy he wonders if somewhere there could be a green rose, green seems to be equated with artistic imagination. But later, Stephen is repelled by steaming pools of green cow dung (again, warmth-wetness, but repulsive). Green here associates itself not only with decay, a significance dwelt upon in *Dubliners* and *Ulysses*, but if we accept the cow-country identification discussed earlier, the color assumes its traditional connection with Ireland. The velvet green back on Aunt Dante's brush stands for Parnell, but in Stephen's dream, Dante, dressed in red and green, spurns Parnell's mourners, as she is subsequently to do at the Christmas table, where the red and green decora-

34

tions, appropriate enough to the season, serve also to remind us of political considerations.

If a green rose is imaginative, a red rose is actual, and red seems to represent various facets of external reality. But the rose in Stephen's vision on the beach is a red one. At the end of the novel, however, as Stephen prepares for his flight, it is the "red-rimmed horny eyes" of the traditionally provincial Irish peasant that Stephen fears most.

In a part-by-part analysis these color images seem at first to form a hopelessly inconsistent conglomeration. But viewed in terms of synthesis and pattern, they seem to serve the same function as the other streams of imagery previously discussed. I have called these patterns "polarities," but Joyce's own phrase, "interrupted pulsations" might better describe them. From this point of view consistency can be ascribed to them. Green, standing variously for country, decay, and imagination, serves as a color texture within which there are clashes. The various shades are essentially incompatible, and Stephen eventually merges in his mind the green of decay with the green of Ireland and takes his own imaginative green to Paris.

We can trace the same antithesis in Joyce's use of red. Momentarily confusing the red rose of his vision with the redness of reality, mistaking vision for context, Stephen finally reorients the red as pertaining to the environment from which he wishes to escape.

The *Portrait*, then, communicates both discursively and nondiscursively. Announcing his themes overtly in discourse, narrative, and dialogue, Joyce also presents a rich texture of rhythm and imagery which serves to reinforce his themes and to enrich them by subtly increasing dimensions and sounding overtones. The *Portrait* is obviously less elaborate in machinery than *Ulysses,* with its framework of epic. The result is that the organization of the *Portrait* tends to be more *sui generis,* and that the novel itself tends toward greater autonomy. Years ago, the art critic Clive Bell coined the fortunate phrase "significant form" to identify the true esthetic test of the work of art. Like all Joyce's writings, the *Portrait* manifests significant form, and the more we ponder the more we are inclined to say that the novel *is* significant form.

4

The "Portrait" and "Chamber Music"

IN ITS PRESENT FORM, the *Portrait* is the third version of the same basic story. The collection of poems known as *Chamber Music* is the first. In narrative, theme, and imagery, these poems adumbrate the same areas of experience to be developed later in *Stephen Hero* and then in the *Portrait.*

Many of the thirty-six poems that comprise *Chamber Music* were apparently written in 1901 and 1902, while Joyce was a student at University College, Dublin. The story of the young poet carrying his roll of manuscripts along the streets of Dublin is a familiar one, as is that of the struggle for and delay in publication, which finally took place in 1907.

The basic themes stated or implied in *Chamber Music* are young love, frustration, alienation and isolation, and finally exile. The reader of the *Portrait* will recognize this pattern.

The thread of continuity in the poems, although occasionally broken, is not difficult to follow. Poem I introduces a personified Love. Nondirected, or possibly introverted, Love walks unawakened beside but not in the river, a symbol that readers of Joyce will recognize as pertaining to life or experience. The setting is musical:

> Strings in the earth and air
> Make music sweet;

> Strings by the river where
> The willows meet.

Later in the poem, we learn that Love is making the music, but the music itself, possibly symbolizing the materials of art, is not differentiated from its surroundings. Love is also undifferentiated at this stage. This amorphous phase of life, experience, and art corresponds closely to the opening lines of the *Portrait*, wherein we are presented with a segment of undifferentiated infantile experience.

In Poem II, Love's object moves murkily into view, much as in the *Portrait* the child Stephen begins to sort out the welter of childhood impressions and experience. Beginning in Poem III, the tone and perspective change as a personalized dramatic speaker is introduced. Objectively querying a "lonely watcher of the skies," the speaker brings us closer to the young Stephen, although we are still outside him. This is analogous to the *Stephen Hero* stage of the *Portrait* story, in which the perspective is external. But in Poem IV, Stephen or his surrogate is revealed as the dramatic speaker. The music moves closer to Love's object, and the final line reveals the shift:

> 'Tis I that am your visitant.

We have now arrived at the final version of the *Portrait*. The perspective is internal, and the stage upon which the dramatic action unfolds is the mind of the speaker.

Poems V–XVI trace the course of young love lyrically through various moods of contemplation, anticipation, separation, reunion, and fulfillment, to a kind of climactic finality. Love has found its object and location:

> O cool and pleasant is the valley
> And there, love, will we stay.

Various "Dewy" images ("night-dew," "pale dew," "From dewy dreams, my soul arise . . .") combine to give a kind of pristine sensuousness to this section, and suggest a parallelism with the dreamlike condition of the unawakened and awakening Stephen in the *Portrait*:

"Towards dawn he awoke. O what sweet music! His soul was all dewy wet."

But this dewiness dries up rather abruptly in Poem XVII, which tells of a rival, just as in the *Portrait* Stephen senses Cranly's rivalry. Stark, spare, without adjectives, it is a bare statement, almost discursive in nature:

> Because your voice was at my side
> I gave him pain,
> Because within my hand I held
> Your hand again.
>
> There is no word nor any sign
> Can make amend—
> He is a stranger to me now
> Who was my friend.

The glow has been abruptly extinguished. The ardor is chilled. The song has been broken off.

Thus the first half of *Chamber Music* embodies a rhythmic pattern of inflation-deflation which, as we have already seen, is fundamentally the rhythmic pattern of the *Portrait*.

The second half of *Chamber Music* reveals the dramatic speaker or proud young lover as he experiences the awareness of competition, the realization of rivalry, brief moods of nostalgia. ("In the dark pine-wood/I would we lay") A feeling of isolation emerges and grows. Isolation is of course a basic theme of the *Portrait* and Joyce's other works; in this connection Poem XXI is instructively analogous:

> He who hath glory lost, nor hath
> Found any soul to fellow his,
> Among his foes in scorn and wrath
> Holding to ancient nobleness,
> That high unconsortable one—
> His love is his companion.

The mood of detachment and isolation deepens. What was before a celebration of love has now become almost a celebration of the passing of love. In Poem XXVIII, the "gentle lady" is advised to:

> Lay aside sadness and sing
> How love that passes is enough.

And in Poem XXX the "celebrating" theme is overtly stated:

> We were grave lovers. Love is past
> That had his sweet hours many a one;
> Welcome to us now at the last
> The ways that we shall go upon.

The same element of rejoicing in self-imposed isolation emerges in the later sections of the *Portrait*. Exile is near.

But for exile, flight is necessary—flight from the island over the sea. And wings symbolize flight. Thus, in Poem XXXV, the speaker contemplates sea and sea birds:

> All day I hear the noise of waters
> Making moan,
> Sad as the sea-bird is, when going
> Forth alone,
> He hears the winds cry to the waters'
> Monotone.

Similarly, Stephen Dedalus in the *Portrait* contemplates birds when planning his flight.

The final and perhaps the most powerful poem, XXXVI, is in the nature of an apocalyptic utterance:

> I hear an army charging upon the land,
> And the thunder of horses plunging, foam
> about their knees:
> Arrogant, in black armour, behind them stand,
> Disdaining the reins, with fluttering whips,
> the charioteers.

This supernatural army, bursting suddenly upon us, functions in much the same way as the apparition of the "hawklike man flying sunward over the sea" in the *Portrait* and, more specifically, as the diary entry in the closing passages of the novel:

> April 16. Away! Away!

The spell of arms and voices: the white arms of roads, their promise of close embraces and the black arms of tall ships that stand against the moon, their tale of distant nations. They are held out to say: We are alone—come. And the voices say with them: We are your kinsmen. And the air is thick with their company as they call to me, their kinsman, making ready to go, shaking the wings of their exultant and terrible youth.

The analogy between these three apparitions is not one of content—army, hawklike man, the spell of arms and voices—but is rather one of function, tone, and mood. The function is galvanic, the tone involves a thickening of the air, and the mood is one of highest urgency. Flight is imminent.

The foregoing analysis of *Chamber Music* has been a fragmentary one. On one hand, I have not attempted to trace in detail the numerous subsidiary analogies of theme, image, symbol, and rhythm between the poems and the novel. On the other hand, I have not pressed for an exact part-to-part correspondence—in many instances it simply does not exist. At the time, this basic pattern was slowly emerging out of the young Joyce's life and into his art, and the poems were not written to fill in a preconceived outline. It is clear, however, that in broad outline and with variations *Chamber Music* is a shadowy early version of the *Portrait*.

5

The "Portrait" and "Stephen Hero"

THE PROSE antecedent to the *Portrait* is the *Stephen Hero* manuscript, whose date or dates of composition cannot be definitely determined. Precise dating is not essential for our purpose, and it may be assumed that the work was in various stages of progress, either in Joyce's mind or on paper, between 1901 and 1906, with most of the writing having been done in 1904.

The extant manuscript is less than half the length of the original, which apparently ran about a thousand pages, and the fate of the missing section is unknown. One persistent story is that Joyce burned it in despair after many rejections by publishers.

The relationship between *Stephen Hero* and the *Portrait* is complex. A pronounced difference in tone is evident between the two versions. Also, a marked increase in Joyce's creative and technical powers is clearly manifested in the *Portrait,* which is a substantially greater artistic achievement than *Stephen Hero.* The reasons for these differences are not clear, but I shall attempt to come to grips with them after comparing and contrasting the two works.

The surface differences between *Stephen Hero* and the *Portrait* are considerable. First, the extant part of the *Stephen Hero* manuscript covers a period of approximately two years in Stephen's life—his days at the University—whereas the *Portrait* at least adumbrates the first twenty years of his life. Thus the entire *Stephen Hero* story is confined to the period covered in Chapter V of the *Portrait*.

Stephen's contemporaries are sketched in considerably greater detail in *Stephen Hero*. Lynch, Cranly, and others stand forth as characters in their own right, rather than as the shadowy foils of the *Portrait*. But Stephen still conducts and dominates interminable discussions with them on art, morals, religion, and marriage. And as in the *Portrait,* so in *Stephen Hero*, these contemporaries still function as agents of deflation and alienation. After a prolonged discourse by Stephen on esthetics, Cranly meditates and offers a profound remark: "I wonder did that bloody boat, the Sea Queen ever start?" Stephen senses his increasing alienation from Cranly:

> He fancied moreover that he detected in Cranly's attitude towards him a certain hostility, arising out of a thwarted desire to imitate. . . . He no longer . . . sought his friend's opinion or allowed the sour dissatisfaction of his friend's moods to weigh against him. He was egotistically determined that . . . no bond of association or impulse or tradition should hinder him from working out the enigma of his position in his own way.

Emma Clery, Stephen's inamorata, is also seen at much closer range in *Stephen Hero*. His attitude toward her is one of arrogance and condescension. Her attraction for him is entirely physical; to him, "her body seemed so compact of pleasure." But her "loud forced manners shocked him at first until his mind had thoroughly mastered the stupidity of hers." He felt, however, that "even that warm ample body could hardly compensate him for her distressing pertness and middle-class affectations."

Because of her, Stephen for a time attends meetings of the Gaelic League, but he is an unwilling and unsympathetic student of Irish nationalism. He becomes suspicious of her interest in Father Moran, and eventually drops out of the league. He continues to view her as being monocotyledonous:

> He remembered almost every word she had said from the first time he had met her and he strove to recall any word which revealed the presence of a spiritual principle in her worthy of so significant a name as soul. He submitted himself to the perfumes of her body and strove to locate a spiritual principle in it: but he could not.

He resents Emma's claim on his emotions, and decides that he must sever the connection: "At every step that they took Stephen's resolution to leave her and see no more of her became more deeply rooted. Even as a diversion her company was slightly degrading to his sense of dignity." Clearly, he regards her as a potential whore: "The warmth of her body seemed to flow into his, and without a moment's hesitation he put his hand into his pocket and began to finger out his coins."

But the claims of the body and his loneliness clamor persistently, refusing to be ignored. Catching sight of Emma from a window during his Italian lesson, Stephen rushes after her, overtakes her, and confronts her with an abrupt request for one night of love. This galvanizing glimpse of Emma from the window constitutes the first in a series of climactic visions for Stephen. It is the antecedent both of his vision of the girl on the beach in the *Portrait* and of his vision of the light in Molly Bloom's window in *Ulysses*. Here the contrast between this earlier work and the two later ones is clear in terms of Stephen's own esthetic. Improper art, as he declares in the *Portrait,* is kinetic, and results in emotions of desire and loathing, whereas proper art induces static contemplation. Thus there is a revealing difference between Stephen's headlong rush to overtake his vision in *Stephen Hero* and his contemplative reactions to his later visions. It is also interesting to note, in this connection, the changes in perspective and relationship of viewer to viewed in these three epiphanies. In *Stephen Hero,* Stephen is inside and the girl is outside. In the *Portrait,* they are both outside. In *Ulysses,* Stephen is outside and Molly is inside. Perhaps this indicates or parallels the progressive distancing and increasing impersonality of Joyce's concept of Stephen.

To return to Stephen's proposition to Emma—shocked, she refuses him, and their relationship quickly deteriorates thereafter. His final feelings toward her are ambiguous. At the end of *Stephen Hero,* he announces flatly to Lynch: "She is nothing to me now, you know." To which Lynch promptly retorts: "I don't believe that, let me tell you."

In addition to Emma Clery, the members of Stephen's family are given more individual attention in *Stephen Hero* than in the *Portrait.* We learn of his younger brother Maurice, on whom, in the course of evening strolls, Stephen tries out his ideas. Similarly, his dying sister Isabel is presented in some detail. With her waning and death, there is a poignant description of the mood and sense of futility and decay which are so prevalent in *Dubliners.* And Isabel's funeral is clearly a forerunner of Paddy Dignam's burial scene in *Ulysses.*

Stephen's mother is also a more clearly drawn figure in this earlier version of the *Portrait.* He discusses Ibsen with her at length in his determined but futile effort to interest his family in the artistic achievements of the Norwegian dramatist. And Stephen's dispute with his mother about his Easter duty, mentioned only in retrospect in the *Portrait,* is acted out in *Stephen Hero.*

Because of the concentration on one period of Stephen's life, the earlier work also shows us more of his father than does the *Portrait.* But the relationship between Stephen and his parents is essentially the same in both versions. Compare the "abyss of temperament" that separates him from them in the *Portrait* with the following passage from *Stephen Hero:* "He avoided his father sedulously because he now regarded his father's

45

presumptions as the most deadly part of a tyranny, internal and external, which he determined to combat with might and main. He argued no further with his mother, so long as she chose to set the shadow of a clergyman between her nature and his."

If relationships are fundamentally unchanged in the two versions, so are themes. Isolation, exile, and the development of the artist are motifs common to both. In Stephen's discussion of religion with Cranly we see the first flush of rebellion, the necessity of escape, the seeds of the *non serviam* doctrine. Later, still with Cranly, the statement becomes more overt:

> —There is no reason why life should lose all grace and nobility even though Columbus discovered America. I will live a free and noble life.—
> —Yes?—
> —My art will proceed from a free and noble source. It is too troublesome for me to adopt the manners of these slaves. I refuse to be terrorized into stupidity.

The same determination finds its way into later discourse:

> The spectacle of the world in thrall filled him with the fire of courage. He, at least, though living at the farthest remove from the center of European culture, marooned on an island in the ocean, though inheriting a will broken by doubt and a soul the steadfastness of whose hate became as weak as water in siren arms, would live his own life according to what he recognized as the voice of a new humanity, active, unafraid, and unashamed.

This resolution, of course, increases his isolation, and he confesses to Emma: "I live such a strange life—without help or sympathy from anyone."

Stephen's concentration on art and artistic matters is, if anything, more intense and pronounced in *Stephen Hero* than in the *Portrait*. Early in the narrative we learn that he is writing a great deal of verse and that, in lieu of any better alternative, his verse allows him to "combine the offices of penitent and confessor." He puts his lines together letter by letter: "He read Blake and Rimbaud on the values of letters and even permuted and combined the five vowels to construct cries for primitive emotions. To none of his former fervours had he given himself with such a whole heart as to this fervour; the monk now seemed to him no more than half the artist." To achieve this life of art, Stephen feels that exile is not only inevitable but necessary; as he points out to his brother Maurice, "Isolation is the first principle of artistic economy."

As to the product of this devotional life of artistic economy, we are offered the following example:

The dawn awakes with tremulous alarm,
　　How grey, how cold, how bare!
O, hold me still white arms, encircling arms!
　　And hide me, heavy hair!

Life is a dream, a dream. The hour is done
　　And antiphon is said.
We go from the light and falsehood of the sun
　　To bleak wastes of the dead.

This poem of regression might have been written by the young Yeats, except that he would have written it better.

Dante's *Vita Nuova* suggests to Stephen the possibility of a "wreath of verses," and toward this he bends his efforts: "His love-verses gave him pleasure: he wrote them at long intervals and when he wrote it was always a mature and reasoned emotion which urged him." He is conscious of the seeming incongruity of "feudal" terminology employed by a skeptic, but he feels that this relativistic use of language is peculiarly modern and rather pleasing.

Increasingly conscious of his vocation, he tends to view life, emotion, and experience as being important only as grist for his mill: ". . . I do not idealize the girls I see every day. I regard them as marsupials. . . . But still I must express my nature."

To Stephen, dedication implies formulation, and his esthetic doctrine is to him not only explanation but justification. Although certain aspects of the subject are treated in discussions with Maurice and Cranly, the main body of the doctrine is developed in discourse and exposition. Stephen reads an essay on the subject to a literary society. This is in significant contrast to the method employed in the *Portrait,* wherein most of Stephen's esthetic theories are condensed and embodied in dialogue.

The doctrine is essentially the same in both versions, but there are changes in emphasis from one to the other. Stephen separates the beautiful and the good in both instances, and affirms the esthetic end of art and his abhorrence of the "profanity" or "antique principle that the end of art is to instruct, to elevate, and to amuse." In *Stephen Hero,* however, he expands upon the function and position of the artist:

> In fine the truth is not that the artist requires a document of license from the householders entitling him to proceed in this or that fashion but that every age must look for its sanction to its poets and philosophers. The poet is the intense centre of the life of his age to which he stands in a relation than which none can be more vital. He alone is capable of absorbing in himself the life that surrounds him and of flinging it abroad again amid planetary music.

The artist, he continues, is a mediator between the world of his experience and the world of his dreams, and is gifted with two faculties: the selective and the reproductive. Artistic success is achieved in the equating of these faculties. "This perfect coincidence of the two artistic faculties Stephen called poetry."

He now differentiates between the classical and romantic tempers, and extols the classical:

48

A classical style, he said, is the syllogism of art, the only legitimate process from one world to another. Classicism is not the manner of any fixed age or of any fixed country: it is a constant state of the artistic mind. It is a temper of security and satisfaction and patience. The romantic temper, so often and so grievously misinterpreted and not more by others than by its own, is an insecure, unsatisfied, impatient temper which sees no fit abode here for its ideals and chooses therefore to behold them under insensible figures. As a result of this choice it comes to disregard certain limitations. Its figures are blown to wild adventures, lacking the gravity of solid bodies, and the mind that has conceived them ends by disowning them. The classical temper on the other hand, ever mindful of limitations, chooses rather to bend upon these present things and so to work upon them and fashion them that the quick intelligence may go beyond them to their meaning which is still unuttered. In this method the sane and joyful spirit issues forth and achieves imperishable perfection, nature assisting with her goodwill and thanks. For as long as this place in nature is given us it is right that art should do no violence to the gift.

Perhaps the most notable difference between the two versions, in the field of esthetic theory, concerns the doctrine of epiphany, or "showing forth." Implied in the *Portrait*, it is stated in *Stephen Hero*. Stephen, passing through Eccles Street on a misty evening, sees a young lady standing on the steps "of one of those brown brick houses which seem the very incarnation of Irish paralysis." A young man stands below her, and Stephen overhears a relatively meaningless fragment of their conversation:

The Young Lady—(drawling discreetly) . . . O, Yes . . . I was . . . at the . . . cha . . . pel. . . .

The Young Gentleman—(inaudibly) . . . I
. . . (again inaudibly) . . . I . . .

The Young Lady—(softly) . . . O . . . but
you're . . . ve . . . ry . . . wick . . . ed. . . .

This triviality made him think of collecting many
such moments together in a book of epiphanies. By
an epiphany he meant a sudden spiritual manifestation, whether in the vulgarity of speech or of
gesture or in a memorable phase of the mind itself.
He believed that it was for the man of letters to
record these epiphanies with extreme care, seeing
that they themselves are the most delicate and
evanescent of moments.

Stephen explains to Cranly that epiphany results when
the spiritual eye adjusts its vision to an exact focus. He
equates epiphany with Aquinas' third element of beauty
—radiance. But the first two elements of beauty are
here translated "integrity" and "symmetry," instead of
the "wholeness" and "harmony" of the *Portrait*. However,
their meanings are essentially the same. First comes the
synthesis, the separation of object and non-object, which
is integrity. Secondly, as a result of analysis, the relation
of part to part—symmetry—is perceived. And finally,
quidditas is manifested, and *quidditas* embodies radiance—the moment of epiphany. "Its soul, its whatness,
leaps to us from the vestment of its appearance."

More basic than the foregoing points of similarity and
contrast in the two versions is the pronounced change of
tone that occurred from the earlier to the later. Clearly,
Joyce's attitude toward his hero is substantially different
in the *Portrait* from what it was in *Stephen Hero*. His
attitude toward Stephen in the *Portrait* will be studied
later, but it is pertinent now to ascertain the attitude in
Stephen Hero.

At first glance we are inclined to ascribe a certain
objectivity to Joyce's presentation of his earlier hero.
There seems to be more of a reportorial quality in *Stephen Hero*. Closer inspection tends to destroy this illu-

sion, for it becomes increasingly apparent that the narrative is heavily slanted in Stephen's favor by the persistent and frequent use of charged language. This device is used mildly at first:

> People seemed to him strangely ignorant of the values of the words they used so glibly. And pace by pace as this indignity of life forced itself upon him he became enamoured of an idealizing, a more veritably human tradition. The phenomenon seemed to him a grave one and he began to see that people had leagued themselves together in a conspiracy of ignobility and that Destiny had scornfully reduced her prices for them. He desired no such reduction for himself, and preferred to serve her on the ancient terms.

Here, in addition to certain loaded terms, we see the device unfolding in the form of question begging. Instead of being given the opportunity to see this "conspiracy of ignobility" for which "Destiny had scornfully reduced her price," we are told that Stephen had begun to see it. And surely the final sentences, in which Stephen desires no reduction of price for himself, and prefers to serve Destiny "on the ancient terms," strike a rather pronounced heroic attitude that is hardly in keeping with objectivity.

Stephen Hero is peppered with passages of this kind. We learn that "Almost every incident of the day was a goad for him," but we do not witness the incidents. His attitude toward religion is characteristically expressed: "Already while that fever-fit of holiness lay upon him he had encountered but out of charity had declined to penetrate disillusioning forces . . . the most that devotional exercises could do for him was to soothe him. This soothing he badly needed for he suffered greatly from contact with his new environment."

In matters of art the same tone is evident: "The burgher notion of the poet Byron in undress pouring out verses just as a city fountain pours out water seemed to him characteristic of most popular judgments on esthetic matters. . . ." We learn that Stephen is not attaching himself to art "in any spirit of youthful dilettantism," but rather strives "to pierce to the significant heart of everything." In his studies, he finds the unnamed treatises that are assigned to him to be "useless and trifling." When he protests against *Othello,* the young men in the class laugh at him, and Stephen, "as he looked contemptuously at the laughing faces, thought of a self-submersive reptile." Queried by an "idea-proof" young man as to whether he is an artist, and if so why does he not wear his hair long, Stephen wonders "for which of the learned professions the young man's father designed him." To all his critics, Stephen flings "disdain from flashing antlers," another instance of the heroic attitude.

Perhaps the most revealing comments on Stephen are those summarizing his situation and his beliefs:

> He was an enigmatic figure in the midst of his shivering society where he enjoyed a reputation. His comrades hardly knew how far to venture with him as professors pretended to think his seriousness a sufficient warrant against any practical disobedience.

And:

> He spurned from before him the stale maxims of the Jesuits and he swore an oath that they should never establish over him an ascendancy. He spurned from before him a world of the higher culture in which there was neither scholarship nor art nor dignity of manners—a world of trivial intrigues and trivial triumphs. Above all he spurned from before him the company of decrepit youth—and he swore an oath that never would they establish with him a compact of fraud. Fine words! Fine oaths! crying bravely and passionately even in the teeth of circumstances.

In these two passages such loaded terms as "enigmatic," "shivering," "pretended," "spurned," "stale," "trivial," and "decrepit," as well as the over-all tone, are designed to carry the burden of proof or demonstration.

Another category in which *Stephen Hero* fails to achieve objectivity is in that of Stephen's favorite pastime—gulling and galling the Philistines. He always wins the arguments and emerges triumphant. His discussion with the president of the college about the censorship of Stephen's essay on esthetics, his arguments with McCann and Madden on Irish affairs, and his discussion of his Easter duty with his mother, are all examples. The picture is that of a young, heavy-handed, deck-stacking Socrates with spurs.

Emerging from all this is the realization that what we see here is not objectivity but rather a pseudo-objectivity that is in fact highly subjective. Several commentators in the past have referred to the "reportorial" and "dramatic" quality of *Stephen Hero*. It is certainly true that there is more dramatic machinery available in *Stephen Hero* because of the fact that the presentations of the other characters are more complete and externalized. But the quality of *Stephen Hero* is not reportorial but editorial, and the essence of drama—objectivity—is missing, so that what we have in *Stephen Hero,* it seems to me, is not so much drama as self-dramatization. Stephen is continually involved in one process of self-dramatization or another.

Self-dramatization implies self-pity, and certainly this quality is abundantly present in the narrative. Every incident is a goad to Stephen, every experience painful. He complains that he lives "such a strange life—without help or sympathy from anyone." Clearly, some of his lacerations are self-inflicted, and Stephen, by feeling sorry for himself, relieves us of the obligation.

Our sympathy for Stephen is further reduced by his extreme arrogance. We have seen many examples of this already. I offer one more. Madden, attempting unsuccessfully to write poetry, shows the mawkish product to Stephen, who returns it without comment but with this private observation: "When a demand for intelligent sympathy goes unanswered he is a too stern disciplinarian who blames himself for having offered a dullard an opportunity to participate in the warmer movement of a more highly organized life." The arrogance of Stephen, as he is presented in *Stephen Hero,* borders on complete egocentricity, and it is difficult if not impossible to conjure up any feelings of warmth, sympathy, or affection for him.

A story constructed subjectively around such a hero, then, is not likely to function effectively as drama. Throughout the narrative there is the attempt, by means of the devices discussed above, to make up our minds for us, and this is not the climate of drama. Interestingly enough, we find this same subjective tone in Joyce's play *Exiles.* Richard Rowan, it seems to me, stems directly from the Stephen of *Stephen Hero.* This may explain, in part, the dramatic weakness of the play— again, what is achieved is not drama but self-dramatization.

The dramatic weakness of *Stephen Hero* can perhaps be seen most clearly in the pool-room scene, in which Stephen and Cranly watch two clerks play billiards with their superior:

> The hopeless pretence of those three lives before him, their unredeemable servility, made the back of Stephen's eyes feel burning hot. He laid his hand on Cranly's shoulder and said impetuously:
>
> —We must go out at once, I can't stand it any longer—
>
> They crossed the room together and Stephen said:
>
> —If I had remained another minute I think I would have begun to cry—
>
> —Yes, it is bloody awful, said Cranly—
>
> —O, hopeless! hopeless! said Stephen clenching his fists.

Here, our opinions are being forced. In effect we are

being told, by Joyce through Stephen, that we should react as Stephen does. But in the scene preceding this we are presented only with a matter-of-fact description of the participants of the game. There is no "objective correlative." To borrow T. S. Eliot's phrase about Hamlet, Stephen's emotion seems everywhere in excess of the facts. The result is that his vision of horror does not become *our* vision.

In addition to the subjective tone, there is another weakness in *Stephen Hero:* in the writing itself. Many passages seem ponderous, turgid, and dull. Consider these examples:

> This recognition of the beautiful in virtue of the most abstract relations afforded by an object to which the term could be applied so far from giving any support to a commandment of *Noli tangere* was itself no more than a just sequence from the taking off of all interdictions from the artist.

And:

> He had promised himself arguing from the alienated attitudes and half-deferential half-words of pressmen at the mention of the name, a certain extravagance, perhaps an anomalous torridity of the North and though the name beneath Ibsen's photograph never failed to reawaken his sense of wonder, the upright line of the 'b' running so strangely beside the initial letter as to suspend the mind amid incertitudes for some oblivious instants, the final impression made upon him by the figure to which the name was affixed, a figure which he associated with a solicitor's or a stockbroker's office in Dame St., was an impression of relief mixed with disappointment, the relief for his son's sake prevailing dutifully over his own slight but real disappointment.

And:

> This mood of indignation which was not guiltless of a certain superficiality was undoubtedly due to

55

the excitement of release and it was hardly countenanced by them before he realized the dangers of being a demagogue. The attitude which was constitutional with him was a silent, self-occupied, contemptuous manner and his intelligence, moreover, persuaded him that the tomahawk, as an effective instrument of warfare, had become obsolete. He acknowledged to himself in honest egoism that he could not take to heart the distress of a nation, the soul of which was antipathetic to his own, so bitterly as the indignity of a bad line of verse: but at the same time he was nothing in the world so little as an amateur artist.

In addition, there are interminable and ponderous discussions of, and discourses on, the state of Ireland, the evils of Catholicism, and matters of art and artists.

The considerable superiority of the *Portrait*, by comparison, seems everywhere evident. Clearly, in the process of condensation, distillation, and pruning, all the nonessentials have been removed. This process, itself a kind of epiphany, results in a novel that deals in essences rather than externals. The perspective is now interior. Stephen's consciousness holds the center of the stage. Necessarily then, the other characters are more ethereal; their impact on Stephen's mind is now important. In this drama of the mind, for that is essentially what the *Portrait* is, more of Joyce's material is embodied than is true in *Stephen Hero*, where the presentation tends toward exposition. As has been seen, in the *Portrait* the central ideas or themes are presented nondiscursively, by image and rhythm, as well as discursively. This embodiment results in, or is caused by, a marked change of tone in the *Portrait*. Less sheltered by the devices in *Stephen Hero*, Stephen now stands alone, and his ideas are more directly exposed to the buffetings of external realities.

To say that the perspective is internal in the *Portrait* would seem to imply that this novel is more subjective than *Stephen Hero*. Paradoxically, greater objectivity is achieved by this shift, Joyce approaches closer to the mode of drama in the *Portrait* than he does in *Stephen Hero*. Stephen's consciousness is, in the *Portrait*, the stage on which the dramatic action unfolds. This action consists of the struggle for supremacy, or at least ascendancy, between the "three nets" on the one hand, and Stephen's vocation on the other. Viewed in this manner, the novel seems rich in dramatic content. The religious retreat comes quickly to mind. In this drama of hell, Stephen's mind-soul is the protagonist, Father Arnall's sermon the antagonist, and the dramatic action unfolds against a backdrop of the mundane complacency of Stephen's contemporaries. Similarly, in the climactic episode on the beach, we witness the dramatic vocation, symbolized by the apparition of the hawklike man and by the girl, against the sordidness of external reality, represented by the boys on the beach, with Stephen's own doubts and fears functioning as chorus.

The measureable superiority of the *Portrait* over *Stephen Hero* becomes remarkable when we consider the fact that there was almost, if not indeed, a chronological overlap of the two versions.[1] How Joyce was able to return so soon to the same material and to treat it so differently and so much more successfully is a question to which there is no clear answer.

It is interesting, however, to speculate about this. At about the time Joyce went into full swing on the final version of the *Portrait*, he was adding the final stories to *Dubliners*, notably the last and finest, "The Dead." This remarkable story represents a considerable advance over the earlier ones. One of the most apparent things about not only "The Dead" but the other later stories in *Dubliners* is the extent to which visual effects are used. Once we realize this, we are immediately struck by a similar contrast between the *Portrait* and *Stephen Hero*. In the *Portrait*, much of the fundamental content is presented visually, rather than discursively, as in *Stephen Hero*.

It seems that Joyce's technical mastery grew along with his visual imagination. However, there may be a specific reason for his shift of attack; and I shall suggest in a later chapter that this might have derived from his interest in the motion picture.

Regardless of the reason, however, the important consideration is that Joyce somehow made a remarkable advance from *Stephen Hero* to the *Portrait*, for it is in this final version that he comes of age artistically, and confirms on a larger scale the achievement of "The Dead."

In the foregoing comparison of the *Portrait* and *Stephen Hero*, it has not been my intention to imply that the latter is without value. This earlier version is valuable as a sketch book or commonplace book is valuable. It gives us much of the raw or unassimilated material of the *Portrait*, and it is an illuminating basis of measurement of Joyce's artistic progress. It is the necessary starting point for a definitive demonstration of artistic assimilation, transmutation, and embodiment. Embodiment, I think, is the key word. The essential difference between the *Portrait* and *Stephen Hero* seems to be that between telling a story and telling *about* a story.

The manuscript of *Stephen Hero* was supposedly rejected twenty times. A thoughtful reading of the work tends to place us on the side of the publishers. Indeed, perhaps we should be grateful to them, for if *Stephen Hero* had been published, we probably would not have had the *Portrait*.

6

The "Portrait" and "Dubliners"

THE SHORT STORIES that make up the collection *Dubliners*
were probably written between 1905 and 1907 and, after
a long and frustrating delay, were finally published in
1914.

To these stories Joyce ascribed a "special odour of
corruption," and in a letter to the publisher added this
comment: "My intention was to write a chapter of the
moral history of my country and I chose Dublin for the
scene because that city seemed to be the centre of
paralysis."

Dubliners has been described and studied in various
ways by Joyce scholars.[1] Some see the stories as epiphanies revealing the frustrations and defeats of modern
life. Others emphasize the theme of paralysis running
through the stories. Some have, with perhaps excessive
ingenuity, probed the stories for Homeric parallels.[2]

We need not quarrel with these interpretations; we
are interested here in another matter: the relationship
of *Dubliners* to the *Portrait* and, more particularly, the
interpretation of *Dubliners* through the *Portrait*. Thus
we shall be concerned primarily with those aspects of
the stories which most clearly reveal their relationship
to the *Portrait*.

The image or idea that organically connects the short
stories to the novel is, it seems to me, that of the three
nets. Stephen in the *Portrait*, it will be remembered,

identifies these nets: "When the soul of a man is born in this country there are nets flung at it to hold it back from flight. You talk to me of nationality, language, religion. I shall try to fly by those nets." The image of the nets inevitably suggests related or consequent ideas. One of these is paralysis, which as Joyce and Joyce scholars have pointed out, is one of the key themes of *Dubliners*. But there is another related idea which I think is even more important—captivity. The two are not quite the same, and the difference, though apparently slight, is essential. Captivity presupposes an active restraining force, and here may be directly equated with the three nets Stephen fears and seeks to elude. Language, nationality, and religion are captors—agents of confinement, restraint, frustration. Captivity *results* in paralysis. Thus the relationship between the two ideas is one of cause and effect.

If the *Portrait* tells the story of Stephen's battle with the three nets and his attempted escape from them, *Dubliners* tells of those who did not escape. Further, among those captives may be found various projections of Stephen and his condition if he had not fled the nets.

We are introduced to captivity, paralysis, and the nets early in "The Sisters," the opening story of *Dubliners*. This story concerns the death of the eccentric priest Father Flynn and its impact on the boy he had befriended and to whom he had acted as a substitute father. At the outset we see the boy gazing up at the window of the room in which Father Flynn lies dying after his third stroke:

> Every night as I gazed up at the window I said softly to myself the word paralysis. It had always sounded strangely in my ears, like the word gnomon in the Euclid and the word simony in the Catechism. But now it sounded to me like the name of some malificent and sinful being. It filled me with fear, and yet I longed to be nearer to it and to look upon its deadly work.

This paralyzed priest with his stained vestments that have a "green faded look" and the oblique reference to simony clearly connote the net of religion; perhaps the connotation may be broadened to include nationality. We have already seen how Joyce has used "green" imagery in at least three different senses in the *Portrait*, and here the "green faded look" seems to suggest not only decay but decayed Ireland. The theme of nationality is further implied in the insensitive, conformist, and anti-intellectual remarks of Mr. Cotter and the boy's uncle, as is the matriarchal state of the nation by the roles of the boy's aunt and the sisters.

Also in "The Sisters" we find the first projection of Stephen if he had remained in Dublin all his life. Clearly, there are analogies between Father Flynn and Stephen as we know him. The boy reads the card announcing the death of the priest:

July 1st, 1895

The Rev. James Flynn (formerly of S. Catherine's Church, Meath Street), aged sixty-five years.

R.I.P.

We are reminded here of the passage in the *Portrait* wherein Stephen contemplates a priestly vocation. We may also be quite confident that Father Flynn's first name was not idly chosen.

There are other indications that this priest is a projection of Stephen. We learn that the priest was "too scrupulous always," that the "duties of the priesthood was too much for him," that "his life was, you might say, crossed," and that he was "a disappointed man." After he breaks the chalice, he begins to "mope by himself, talking to no one and wandering about by himself." He is finally found alone in the dark in his confession box, "Wide-awake and laughing-like softly to himself." This final vision of dementia serves as a horrifying projection of Stephen's possible condition if he had remained in Ireland and accepted the vocation to which he was by his nature unsuited.

In "The Sisters" the idea of captivity is strongly suggested by narrative and imagery. The priest is a captive of the Church; the Church is the captive of, or is paralyzed by, decay and corruption. "Paralysis" and "simony" are linked in the boy's mind. Ireland is a captive of the matriarchy. The sisters, performing religiously significant rituals, such as serving wine and biscuits, have usurped the function of the priesthood. And the fatherless boy is a captive not only of his aunt and uncle but of the dead priest, as he was of the living priest. Mr. Cotter's warning that a young boy should "run about and play with lads of his own age" indicates that the boy has spent a great deal of time with the priest. He cannot rid himself of the presence of the paralytic, even in the sanctuary of his own room: "But the grey face still followed me. It murmured; and I understood that it desired to confess something. I felt my soul receding into some pleasant and vicious region; and there again I found it waiting for me." The boy finds himself arrested and frustrated by the card announcing the death of the priest. "The reading of the card persuaded me that he was dead and I was disturbed to find myself at check."

The dominant images of "The Sisters" are invariably those of confinement. The "lighted square of window" behind which the paralytic priest is dying, the boy's room in which the vision of the priest pursues him, the priest's coffin, the "little room downstairs" in which the boy and the women gather for a kind of communion after the priest's death—all suggest restraint or captivity. And these images prepare us for the final image of ultimate captivity, the confession box in which the priest had been discovered laughing softly to himself in the dark.

"An Encounter," essentially a story of initiation, represents the first attempt at escape from the nets. The word "escape" appears several times in this study of an excursion of two young truants which, significantly enough, is frustrated short of its goal.

At the waterfront the two boys see a Norwegian ship and a sailor with green eyes. The "green" motif here seems to suggest creativity and imagination, as the ship from Norway suggests Ibsen, for whom Joyce, through Stephen, has expressed great admiration. But creative green changes to sinister green as the boys later encounter the perverted stranger who has a pair of "bottle-green eyes." In this felicitous phrase we have the suggestion not only of decaying Ireland but of imbibing Ireland, and the stranger, with his talk of whipping, reminds us of the pandybat episode of the *Portrait,* and thus of perverted authority, an aspect of the net of nationality. The man terrifies the boy, who at the end of the story, shouts for his comrade: "How my heart beat as he came running across the field to me! He ran as if to bring me aid. And I was penitent; for in my heart I had always despised him a little." The boy shrinks back before the vision of the stranger, and returns to the fold defeated. Escape changes to retreat.

The nature of the stranger suggests that the story is one of initiation. The two boys have attempted an escape toward a realm of fantasy fulfillment, in which motifs of the "Wild West" and the Norwegian sailing ship represent a romantic pseudo-reality. But actuality confronts them in the disturbing presence of the green-eyed man. Suggesting reality, disorder, and evil, this perverted stranger, with the "great gaps in his mouth between his yellow teeth," stands as a potential captor. That he himself is captive of his own condition is clear when we learn that "his mind was circling round and round in the same orbit." We are later to be confronted with this same image of circular captivity in the delineation of Gabriel Conroy's situation in "The Dead."

"Araby," another story of initiation, also represents an attempted but frustrated escape in the form of a defeated quest. Infatuated with a neighbor girl, the boy journeys to a bazaar named Araby to bring back a gift for her. But he is delayed by the thoughtlessness of his uncle, and arrives at the bazaar too late to purchase anything of value. The story ends as he gazes into the darkness, seeing himself a creature "driven and derided by vanity," his eyes burning "with anguish and anger." This moment of self-realization climaxes an exceptionally rich story in which all three nets are indicated. The name "Araby" suggests an escape from the Church: the boy's aunt hopes that it is not "some Freemason affair." And the name casts an "Eastern enchantment" over the boy, and in this aspect seems to stand for romance and imagination. The boy's uncle, with his unfeeling sententiousness, suggests, as in "The Sisters," Ireland. Characteristically, having forgotten that the boy had planned a trip to the bazaar, he arrives home so late that the project is almost abandoned.

The net of language is treated specifically for the first time in "Araby." There seem to be two categories to this net. One implies a close association with nationality: we recall Stephen's sporadic attendance at, and disgust with, the Gaelic League. The other category involves *use* of language and Stephen's dedication to its creative use. The contrast between the boy's language and the language that surrounds him is graphically depicted in "Araby":

We walked through the flaring streets, jostled by drunken men and bargaining women, amid the curses of labourers, the shrill litanies of shop-boys who stood on guard by the barrels of pigs' cheeks, the nasal chanting of street-singers, who sang a *come-all-you* about O'Donovan Rossa, or a ballad about the troubles in our native land. These noises converged in a single sensation of life for me: I imagined that I bore my chalice safely through a throng of foes.

This "throng of foes," then, functions as the net of language, which the boy seeks to evade by bearing his chalice safely through. It is interesting to note here that he is attempting to do what the paralyzed priest who broke the chalice in "The Sisters" could not do. Readers of Joyce are well aware of the more determined and frontal assaults he made on this net of language in *Ulysses* and *Finnegans Wake*.

The patterns of "Araby" and "The Encounter" are similar. In each story the young boy pursues his romantic dream but is confronted with reality—a reality with which he is unable to cope and from which he retreats into captivity. In "Araby" we also find various images of confinement that reinforce the meaning of the narrative. The "blind street" on which the boy lives, the "back drawing-room" in which the priest has died, the air itself, "musty from having been long enclosed"— all these images serve to establish the condition of captivity. Significantly, the boy journeys alone to the bazaar in the third-class carriage of a deserted train. The ultimate image—the deserted bazaar hall with its empty stalls—suggests a penitentiary.

In "Eveline" the perspective changes but the theme remains constant. The central character is now a girl, but she too is trapped. In this story the idea of captivity receives one of its most overt statements. During most of the tale she sits looking out her window. As a picture of an unknown priest—a kind of captor—broods over her, she reviews her life. We learn that she is on the verge of eloping to Buenos Aires. Thoughts of her insular father and "the pitiful vision of her mother's life" lay powerful hands on her, goading her toward escape. But at the quay, her lover beckoning her toward the ship, she draws back, suddenly terrified at the thought of freedom. The net is too strong for her to break through: "She set her white face to him, passive, like a helpless animal. Her eyes gave him no sign of love or farewell or recognition." She shrinks back into the captivity of family, country, tradition, and past.

Weaker than the other stories, "After the Race" hints at, but does not clearly convey, definite meaning. The son of a *nouveau riche* Irish butcher mingles with wealthy

Frenchmen and an American. He loses heavily in a game of cards. It is not clear whether this loss will prevent him from going into business with one of the Frenchmen, as his father wants him to do. Perhaps the story is intended to portray the attractiveness but impossibility of escape to a fuller life.

The meaning of "Two Gallants" is clearer. Corley and Lenehan, the two central characters of this ironically titled story, are representative young Dubliners. The plot, such as it is, concerns Corley's attempt to get money from a serving girl to whom he has granted his favor. At the end, he produces a coin triumphantly. The surroundings and the outlooks of the two youths are sordid, and the outlines of the net of nationality are clear. The two men are of contrasting types: Corley is the egotistical and successful lover. Lenehan seems to be another projection of Stephen. His yachting cap and rubber shoes are familiar trappings to us. His eyes twinkle occasionally with "cunning enjoyment," but in repose his face bears a "ravaged look." His conversation is tedious. In short, he is a bore, and he is plainly weary of his lot:

> His tongue was tired for he had been talking all the afternoon in a public house in Dorset Street. Most people considered Lenehan a leech but, in spite of this reputation, his adroitness and eloquence had always prevented his friends from forming any general policy against him. He had a brave manner of coming up to a party of them in a bar and of holding himself nimbly at the borders of the company until he was included in a round. He was a sporting vagrant armed with a vast stock of stories, limericks and riddles.

Parasite, talker, Lenehan is also a voyeur. Corley's purpose with the servant girl is plain, but Lenehan only wants to "get a good look" at her. Both Corley's and Lenehan's lives are sordid and empty, but Lenehan's is sterile as well.

Again, the theme of captivity or capture is implicit

throughout the story. The dominant image is that of a coin—itself a symbol of ransom—which Corley exacts from the captive serving girl. Yet, as in several of the other stories, the captor is also captive. Corley, like the stranger in "The Encounter," is enmeshed in his own net—that of nationality.

Perhaps the most significant passage in "Two Gallants" is that in which Lenehan, an obvious captive of his lot, orders and eats a plate of peas while awaiting Corley's return from the assignation. This isolated incident is not particularly significant in itself, but in context with the *Portrait* it becomes richly meaningful. At the end of the *Portrait*, Stephen, about to depart, meets Emma Clery for the last time: "Talked rapidly of myself and my plans. In the midst of it unluckily I made a sudden gesture of a revolutionary nature. I must have looked like a fellow throwing a handful of peas up into the air." These two lots of peas now suggest pottage and birthrights. Stephen, leaving Ireland, pays his ransom by rejecting the symbol of bondage, and reclaims the birthright that Lenehan, remaining behind, trapped, sells daily. This motif recurs in *Finnegans Wake*, where Shem, acting out the Jacob-Esau pattern, ". . . even ran away with himself and became a farsoonerite, saying he would far sooner muddle through the hash of lentils in Europe than meddle with Irrland's split little pea."

In "The Boarding House," the boarder Mr. Doran seduces Mrs. Mooney's daughter Polly (although apparently the seduction is mutual), and is bulldozed into marrying her by Mrs. Mooney, who is of course aided by social and religious mores and pressures. Mr. Doran seems to be another projection of a settled-down Stephen. We learn that he had sown his share of wild oats as a young man, had boasted of being a freethinker, denying the existence of God to his companions in pubs. "But all that was passed and done with . . . nearly." He is now a respectable and hard-working employee of a wine merchant. (We recall that a clerkship in the brewery was once recommended for Joyce.) Doran resents Polly's bad grammar and her mother's vulgarity, but in the end he takes the only course open to him within the nets. The theme again is entrapment, the rooming house is an image of captivity, and the mother, suggesting Ireland, is the captor.

Little Chandler, the frustrated poet of "A Little Cloud," is another trapped Stephen. Clerk, husband, and father, he conjures up in his mind favorable reviews for books he will never write, and realizes that one "could do nothing in Dublin." The return of Gallaher, a successful journalist, serves to crystallize Chandler's vague discontent and melancholy. He resents Gallaher's vulgarity and success while envying his experience and reputation. Convinced that he could do better if he "had a chance," he returns home and is confronted with the inartistic realities of wife, furniture, and crying baby. Unable to soothe the child, he is shouldered out of the way by his wife and, submitting to matriarchal authority, he steps back into the shadows while she deals expertly with the child. Shame and remorse visit him, and we are left to guess whether the shame is at his inadequacy or at his entrapment.

In "Counterparts" we meet a different version of the trapped family man. Where Little Chandler is meek, Farrington is choleric. Buffeted by a day of defeats, he pawns his watch and seeks his habitual alcoholic solace, reliving his one minor triumph of the day: an impertinent answer to his superior. But he is defeated even in his desire to get drunk—his money runs out. The vision of a plump feminine arm in a pub, together with the defeat of his own in a hand-wrestling contest, goads him into a son-beating rage upon his arrival home. This prisoner revolves in his orbit around places of confinement—office, pub, home. Our sympathies are not so directly involved with Farrington as with Little Chandler, yet we see them both as enmeshed Dubliners.

68

"Clay" concerns a middle-aged spinster named Maria, a cheerful but unfulfilled woman who cooks in a laundry. By name, description, and function she seems to suggest aspects of both nationality and religion. There is a certain witchlike quality about her: when she laughs, her nose and chin almost meet. She is known as a peacemaker, but she cannot establish peace between Joe, whose family she visits on Hallow Eve, and Athy, Joe's estranged brother. She brings a present to the family, but leaves it by mistake on the tram. As Joe often has said of her, "Mamma is mamma but Maria is my true mother." This "true mother" is pressed into a traditional choosing game at Joe's. Blindfolded, her hands touch clay first. But this grim reminder of death, the ultimate captor, is quckly removed and Maria, oblivious, now chooses the prayer book. She is prevailed upon to sing *I Dreamt that I Dwelt,* but she omits the verse about marriage. Joyce closes with an ironic commentary: "But no one tried to show her her mistake, and when she had ended her song, Joe was very much moved. He said that there was no time like the long ago and no music for him like poor old Balfe, whatever other people might say; and his eyes filled up so much with tears that he could not find what he was looking for and in the end he had to ask his wife to tell him where the corkscrew was." If Maria is trapped, she shows no sign of awareness or rebellion, but in her very condition, into which are skillfully blended suggestions of unfulfillment, country, Church, and death, we see the outlines of the nets. And we see also the emergence of a motif to be elaborated on in "The Dead"—the idea of death itself, here symbolized by clay and Maria's living death, as ultimate captivity.

In "A Painful Case" Stephen's surrogate reappears, this time in the form of Mr. James Duffy, a middle-aged celibate whose pride and emotional impoverishment result in self-imposed isolation. In this poignant story he makes friends with a Mrs. Sinico, but when she reveals the extent of her emotional involvement he quickly draws back and they "mutually" agree to break off the alliance. He resumes his solitary ways and, four years later, learns of her degeneration and death. His initial reaction is one of self-justification, but this gives way to a feeling of guilt at having denied or rejected her love. Guilt in turn yields to despair at his own situation, and his final realization is one of his complete aloneness. His is a case history of emotional starvation. We need read only the description of his small, bare, ascetic room to realize that he is a prisoner, barred from the warm richness of the emotional life, one of the living dead, living in a cell.

In "Ivy Day in the Committee Room" the net of nationality is clearly manifest. This colloquy among a group of Irish ward heelers is played against the backdrop of the brooding spirit of the dead Parnell. The sordid realities of vote canvassing and of priests in politics dramatize the gulf between Parnell's ideals and practicality. The story is climaxed by the reading of a mawkish poem about the dead hero, a poem punctuated with popping corks and applauded with beery sentiment.

"A Mother" reintroduces the idea of Irish matriarchy. Mrs. Kearney, who married out of spite and who had been educated in "a high-class convent, where she had learned French and music," brings up her daughter Kathleen in like fashion and then starts promoting and managing the girl's musical career. Joyce here pokes fun at the Irish Revival: "When the Irish Revival began to be appreciable Mrs. Kearney determined to take advantage of her daughter's name and brought an Irish teacher to the house. Kathleen and her sister sent Irish picture postcards to their friends and these friends sent back other Irish postcards." Soon Kathleen is in the thick of social life with musicians and Nationalist friends who are adept enough in the old language to say "goodbye to one another in Irish." Kathleen is offered a job as an accompanist at a series of concerts, and Mrs. Kearney takes over. The concert series is poorly attended, and Mrs. Kearney further disrupts it by staging a sit-down strike, with her daughter as sitter. Using the Revival and the second-rate concert, Joyce jibes at Dublin's cultural pretensions in this story, but the central image is that of the dominating mother—one of the nets. Like the mother in "The Boarding House," she seems to embody Ireland, and functions as a captor imprisoning the spirit of her daughter Kathleen.

If "Ivy Day in the Committee Room" exhibits the net of nationality, "Grace" is its religious counterpart. The story, in the nature of a parody on the *Divine Comedy,* opens with the fall of boozy Tom Kernan down some stairs into a latrine. This fall from grace gives the well-meaning and stanch supporters of the Church Messrs. Power, Cunningham, and McCoy the opportunity to attempt the regeneration of Kernan, who has not attended church for twenty years and who is "fond, moreover, of giving side-thrusts at Catholicism." Kernan's wife is willing that the attempt be made, but skeptical of its outcome: "Religion for her was a habit, and she suspected that a man of her husband's age would not change greatly before death. . . . Her beliefs were not extravagant. She believed steadily in the Sacred Heart as the most generally useful of all Catholic devotions and approved of the sacraments. Her faith was bounded by her kitchen, but, if she was put to it, she could believe also in the banshee and in the Holy Ghost." Conversing on papal infallibility in an atmosphere of genial self-righteousness and liquid cheer in Kernan's bedroom, the salvationists mention a forthcoming Jesuit retreat, to be presided over by Father Purdon. ("Fine jolly fellow! He's a man of the world like ourselves.") They all plan to attend—to "wash the pot together," as Mr. Cunningham puts it. Mr. Kernan, invited with studied casualness, is noncommittal, but when his wife enters the bedroom she is presented with a *fait accompli.* They inform her that they are all going to attend the retreat, her husband included. Mr. Kernan essays a nervous smile and says he does not really mind. A would-be rebel, he thus joins the long list of the trapped in *Dubliners.*

At the retreat Father Purdon climaxes the story as he speaks to a full house of businessmen "in a businesslike way." He proclaims himself their "spiritual accountant," and he asks everyone to "open his books, the books of his spiritual life, and see if they tallied accurately with conscience." The most important thing, he continues, is to be "straight and manly" with God. If their accounts tally, they are to say: "Well, I have verified my accounts. I find all well." But if there are discrepancies, they are to admit it like a man: "Well, I have looked into my accounts, I find this wrong and this wrong. But, with God's grace, I will rectify this and this. I will set right my accounts." Perhaps Joyce in this epiphany—this cosily unspiritual discourse—is, in addition to delineating the net of religion, here exposing the real fall from grace, the real trap.

The final story in the collection—"The Dead"—defies brief analysis. This remarkable work, rated by T. S. Eliot as one of the finest short stories in the English language, reinforces many of the themes of the other stories of *Dubliners.* "The Dead" concerns a Christmas dance given by the Misses Kate and Julia Morkan and attended by their nephew Gabriel Conroy and his wife Gretta among others. After the party Gabriel's desire for his wife is aroused, but she, because of a song she has heard at the party, is grief-stricken at the memory of young Michael Furey, who died for love of her in Galway years earlier. Gabriel's mood changes from frustrated desire and injured pride to acceptance, impersonal understanding, and union with the universal twilight of the soul.

There is at least a shadowy correspondence among "The Dead," "An Encounter," and "Araby." In one sense, "The Dead" is also a story of initiation. Gabriel, like his younger counterpart in the earlier stories, learns something new about his world, and is deflated and defeated by this knowledge. The fundamental patterns of the three stories are thus roughly analogous. But the analogy ceases when Joyce, in his later and much more considerable story, carries Gabriel beyond the point of deflation and defeat to acceptance and understanding.

In one sense, the fundamental action of "The Dead" is a succession of deflations of Gabriel by three women. His expansive hopes for an early marriage for Lily, the serving girl, are met with her bitter retort, "The men that is now is only all palaver and what they can get out of you." Later he is deflated by Miss Ivors, a fervid Nationalist, who calls him a "West Briton." And Gretta's tale of Michael Furey is of course the final deflation.

But to ascribe so limited a theme to this story is to impoverish it. From the title, the ending of the story, and much of what lies between, it seems clear that the over-all theme is death—more particularly, living death. The ambiguity of the snow and the Christmas season, both suggesting life and death as well, hint at the union of life and death which is the essence of the story. And the idea of decay and death is reinforced by frequent references to the superiority of the past, notably in Gabriel's speech at the dinner table. This motif is also present in such stories as "Ivy Day in the Committee Room" and "Clay," and Gabriel's speech in the final story functions as a kind of reprise.

The relationship of "The Dead" to the *Portrait* is clear. First, there is in Gabriel Conroy the most nearly complete projection of Stephen to be found anywhere in *Dubliners*. By description and in attitudes he tallies closely with Stephen as he might have developed had he remained in Dublin. Essentially an unfulfilled man of letters, Gabriel feels superior to his surroundings and writes book reviews mainly so that he can fondle books. In telling and acting out the story of the mill horse who walks interminably in a circle, he is speaking more autobiographically than he knows. His manner is stiff, his conversation is stilted, and his speech on Irish hospitality is stuffy. Near the end of the story, deflated by the tale of Michael Furey, humiliated by the realization that Gretta for years "had been comparing him in her mind with another," Gabriel experiences a bitter moment of self-revelation:

> A shameful consciousness of his own person assailed him. He saw himself as a ludicrous figure, acting as a pennyboy for his aunts, a nervous, well-meaning sentimentalist, orating to vulgarians and idealising his own clownish lusts, the pitiable fatuous fellow he had caught a glimpse of in the mirror. Instinctively he turned his back more to the light lest she see the shame that burned on his forehead.

The other implication of the story which connects it with the *Portrait* is that of the nets. More completely than the other stories, "The Dead" shows life in the nets and, further, shows that this life is a living death.

Every person in the story is a captive. The Misses Morkan are ensnared by the past, Miss Ivors by the net of nationality; the snow, suggesting the ultimate captor—death—broods over and confines all. But with the three principals of the story—Gabriel, Gretta, and Michael Furey—the situation is more complex. I include Michael Furey as a principal character because, although dead, he governs a substantial part of the story. These three characters are mutually involved in two series of highly significant relationships.

The first of these involves captor-captive relationships. Gabriel, in some respects a total image of captivity, is the captive not only of his heritage and emotional poverty but of Gretta. Gretta is at once captor and captive. Gabriel and Michael are her captives, yet she cannot escape from Gabriel; she is also the captive of Michael, and cannot escape from the bonds of her past emotional involvement with him. And Michael is the captive of Gretta and death. He died for love of her, and his coffin represents ultimate confinement.

The second relationship is that between life and death. Death in "The Dead" represents figurative as well as physical lack of life. Gabriel, although physically alive, is emotionally dead. Gretta, once emotionally alive in her relationship with Michael Furey, is now emotionally dead although physically alive. And Michael, once emotionally alive, is now physically dead. Thus Joyce, relating the emotional life to the physical, suggests a vital correspondence between the two. Emotional death becomes living death.

At the end of the story Gabriel achieves a deeper vision and greater awareness of this union of life and death. In one of Joyce's most evocative and memorable passages, which begins with the tap of snow on the window and thus is reminiscent of the gravel Michael Furey used to throw at Gretta's window, Gabriel accepts this union and, moving from the specific to the general, identifies himself and all living with the universal dead. The uniting agent is the snow:

> A few light taps upon the pane made him turn to the window. It had begun to snow again. He watched sleepily the flakes, silver and dark, falling obliquely against the lamplight. The time had come for him to set out on his journey westward. Yes, the newspapers were right: snow was general all over Ireland. It was falling on every part of the dark central plain, on the treeless hills, falling softly upon the Bog of Allen and, farther westward, softly falling into the dark mutinous Shannon waves. It was falling, too, upon every part of the lonely churchyard on the hill where Michael Furey lay buried. It lay thickly drifted on the crooked crosses and headstones, on the spears of the little gate, on the barren thorns. His soul swooned slowly as he heard the snow falling faintly through the universe

and faintly falling, like the descent of their last end, upon all the living and the dead.

Thus Joyce in *Dubliners* cocks a penetrating, understanding, yet ironic eye at the life he has rejected. He views the lives of those who have stayed behind, and delineates the paralysis, decay, and defeats of those lives. He imagines himself still in Dublin, and sketches in the frustrations that would have been in store for him. And over all the glimpses he affords us, we see one superimposed, central, and dominant yet always implicit image—the nets.

Perceiving the ubiquity of the nets in *Dubliners* will illuminate what has been a problem for some Joyce scholars—the motivations of the characters. If we keep the *Portrait* in mind, these motivations are painfully clear—they are the motivations of the trapped. Rebellion against the nets, resignation to them, unthinking acceptance of them, rationalization of them—these make up the motivations. And within the frame of reference that involves not only *Dubliners* but the *Portrait*, they are only too logical.

Although the stories of *Dubliners* are independently meaningful, they are, then, considerably enriched when viewed and interpreted through the *Portrait*. And *Dubliners* in turn gives meaningful background to the *Portrait*. We see in considerably more detail what Stephen is fleeing and why. The two works are mutually and organically concomitant.

7

The "Portrait" and "Ulysses"

THE *Portrait* and *Ulysses* are so closely interconnected as to render impossible a complete catalogue of correspondences within a limited space. The meaning of one involves and reinforces the meaning of the other. It is an impoverishing experience for the reader of both works to attempt to separate them, since each accretes to the other. Certainly our understanding of the Stephen of *Ulysses* would be diminished without the constant echo or undertone of Stephen's background in the *Portrait*. Conversely, the plight of Stephen in the *Portrait* becomes more poignant if we are aware of his condition as revealed in *Ulysses* and thus know that his flight to Paris is doomed to failure. Too, the Stephen-Bloom relationship in *Ulysses* is more meaningful because of Stephen's isolation from and rejection of his father in the *Portrait*. Also, we are prepared for the idea of Molly Bloom as archetypal woman by the Eileen-Emma Clery antecedents. And the reinforcement of Stephen's vision of Molly's window by his earlier vision on the beach in the *Portrait* has been mentioned earlier.

The two works, then, are tightly interconnected and mutually reflexive: we constantly work back and forth between them. In general, their basic relationship to each other may be illustrated as follows:

The smaller of the concentric circles is the microcosm of self represented by the *Portrait,* with its focus on the individual consciousness. In *Ulysses,* the cosmos, the focus is broadened to include modern man. But within each circle, the polarities are the same; or if the circles are changed to spheres, both spheres may be said to revolve on the same axis. At one end of the axis is the self; at the other end, what we may loosely call society. It is this opposition in which Stephen is embroiled throughout both the *Portrait* and *Ulysses.* In the later novel, however, Stephen-Bloom-Molly become a construct of modern man; and what, in the *Portrait,* was primarily Stephen's fight against conformity to preserve his artistic consciousness now becomes, in *Ulysses,* the struggle of modern man to come to terms with the world in which he lives.

Let us examine more specifically the relationship between these two novels. Since the sum total of either work seems to be involved in the reading of the other, it is futile to attempt to unravel all the separate strands that bind them together. There are, however, four representative categories that may be studied with profit. Each of these includes many single strands, and together they serve to link the two works: continuity of theme, certain recurring streams of connected imagery, structural rhythm, and certain aspects of technique—notably the so-called stream of consciousness or interior monologue.

The continuity of themes is obvious. As in the *Portrait,* isolation is the keynote in *Ulysses.* Stephen in *Ulysses* is perhaps even more isolated than he is in the *Portrait,* for he has now realized the futility of his flight. As we see him in the tower at the start of the day with his fellow tenants, Mulligan and Haines, we realize in retrospect the isolation of the Paris experience and the unchanged condition of his life. Later, as we glimpse him teaching at Mr. Deasy's school, wandering along the beach, discoursing on Shakespeare in the library, or even carousing with the medical students, we are emphatically aware that here is a man terribly alone. Even after his meeting and near communion with Bloom, Stephen wanders out into the night alone and his day ends as it began, in isolation.

Stephen is not the only isolated person in *Ulysses;* we have Bloom to consider also. No artist or intellectual, Bloom is in many ways representative of modern man. Perhaps more nearly than any character in fiction, he approaches that mythical entity known as the average man. What happens to this average man? He spends his entire day in complete and near-complete isolation. He prepares breakfast alone, and visits a butcher shop, church, and druggist alone. And although he rides to Paddy Dignam's funeral in company with others, he is completely set apart from them by four considerations. First, he is a Jew. Second, Stephen's father glimpses Stephen enroute, and there is ensuing comment on this unregenerate son. But Bloom's son has died in infancy. Third, Bloom's father was a suicide, and Bloom is in a predominantly Catholic environment. Fourth, we see Blazes Boylan, Molly's lover, and we are thus reminded that Bloom's cuckoldry is another category of rejection and consequent isolation. Bloom wanders through his day alone. Wherever he goes, he is either ignored, barely tolerated, or rejected—in one instance, forcibly ejected. Joyce points to an inglorious symbol as Bloom departs from the pub where he has lunched: "Under the sandwichbell lay on a bier of bread one last, one lonely, last sardine of summer. Bloom alone." Finally, late at night after Stephen has gone, Bloom's isolation achieves cosmic overtones. Alone, he experiences "the cold of inter-stellar space." Bloom now goes to bed, and our final glimpse of him is a graphic one. In the early editions of *Ulysses*, a large dot indicates Bloom's final position, thus:

●

A single finite dot, surrounded by infinite space. His isolation is now complete.

But isolation is not the only theme from the *Portrait* to reappear in *Ulysses*. There is also the idea of the Fall, which combines the failure of the flight into artistic freedom and the lapse from grace. In one sense Stephen falls in the *Portrait*, in another sense he does not. His submission to youthful lusts dramatizes his partial lapse from grace, but the real fall is to come: "The snares of the world were its ways of sin. He would fall. He had not yet fallen but he would fall silently, in an instant." This sense of anticipation of the lapse reappears after Stephen sees the girl on the beach. Now he eagerly awaits it, since it has come to signify to him the necessary ante-cedent to his conversion to earthly beauty and concomi-tant artistic creation: "To live, to err, to fall, to triumph, to recreate life out of life!"

In *Ulysses*, however, Stephen has fallen. The Fall is symbolized by the failure of his flight to Paris, for which he bitterly lacerates himself:

> You were going to do wonders, what? Missionary to Europe after fiery Columbanus. Fiacre and Scotus on their creepystools in heaven spilt from their pintpots, loudlatinlaughing: Euge! Euge! Pre-tending to speak broken English as you dragged your valise, porter threepence, across the slimy pier at Newhaven. *Comment?* Rich booty you brought back; *Le tutu*, five tattered numbers of *Pantalon Blanc et Culotte Rouge*, a blue French telegram, curiosity to show:
> —Mother dying come home father.

And later in the day, in the library, the Fall is recapitulated: "Fabulous artificer, the hawklike man. You flew. Whereto? Newhaven-Dieppe, steerage passenger. Paris and back. Lapwing. Icarus. *Pater, ait.* Seabedabbled, fallen, weltering. Lapwing you are. Lapwing he." About to fall in the *Portrait,* Stephen in *Ulysses* has already fallen. The Fall takes place between the books. The fallen state approximates the state of death, and Stephen throughout *Ulysses* is struggling toward life again. His final meeting with Bloom gives hints of rebirth, but for resurrection itself we must await *Finnegans Wake.*

The falling Icarus cries out to his father. Throughout *Ulysses* Stephen is looking for someone to cry out to. This search for the father, initially postulated in the *Portrait,* is perhaps Joyce's major preoccupation in *Ulysses.* The casting of Stephen in the role of Telemachus, his continuing meditations on the consubstantiality of the son and the father, the many hints, suggestions, and analogies of father-son relationships, his unconvincing but functional theories about Shakespeare —all these combine to make this quest one of the central themes of the book. In the *Portrait* Stephen rejects his nominal father in favor of a fabulous one. This, as he and we have seen, is unsuccessful, and the lesson Stephen learns in *Ulysses*—if indeed he does learn one—is that some sort of communion with mankind, here epitomized by Bloom, is a necessary antecedent to finding the father, also epitomized by Bloom.

In *Ulysses* Stephen is still fighting the battle of the three nets, or, as he now refers to them, the three nooses. He is still determinedly a nonconformist, and dramatizes his credo of *non serviam* by his refusal to kneel and pray at the bedside of his dying mother—the logical climax of his refusal to make his Easter duty at her request in the *Portrait.*

His dead mother in *Ulysses* functions, as his live mother did in the *Portrait,* as an inclusive image of Church and country, and the "agenbite of inwit" that tortures the young intellectual throughout the book clearly has national and spiritual as well as maternal connotations.

Frequent encounters with the nets or nooses are in evidence early in the novel. The appropriate symbol of Irish art, according to Stephen, is the cracked looking glass of a servant. In religious matters, his position is unpleasant but clear to him. He refers to himself as a "horrible example of free thought." Here we see the unproductive and empty result of the rejection of the spiritual in favor of the secular, and the conversion to earthly beauty so glowingly experienced by Stephen on the beach in the *Portrait*.

Irish nationality, according to Stephen, is a state of servitude to two masters, English and Italian—the British state and the Catholic Church. The withered milk woman with shrunken paps in the Telemachus episode, "serving her conqueror and her gay betrayer"—Haines and Mulligan—is a symbol of Ireland. She gives more attention to these two than she does to Stephen. "Me she slights," he muses, suggesting the conflict of Ireland and artist. Significantly, she does not understand her native language when Haines, the foreigner, addresses her in Gaelic, but she is quick to comment, "I'm told it's a grand language by them that knows." But Stephen, as is true also in the *Portrait*, makes no attempt to disguise his opinion of the practitioners of his "grand language" —those involved in the Gaelic and literary revivals.

Perhaps most notable in this area, however, is Joyce's achievement in incorporating all the material of the nets into one suggestive and inclusive complex of thought and feeling, and then bringing it to a focal point and climax. He begins by substituting the image of the nooses for that of the nets. This later image takes us back to the *Portrait* and gathers up, not only the "crossblind" priest who toys with a loop of cord, but all the attendant "hangman" motifs of authority and punishment: the "apologize" jingle about the eagles, the pandybat, and the "submit" theme. The noose image is embodied and reinforced in *Ulysses* in the person of H. Rumbold, master barber and hangman. His letter of application is read in a pub in the Cyclops episode. Its position here is of course functional, as the theme of this episode seems to be a kind of one-eyed vengeance; Bloom, ejected by the irate nationalist citizen, is the victim of one of the nooses. This juxtaposition, in Rumbold, of razor and image of punishment is reminiscent of Mulligan's razor, which lies crossed on the shaving bowl at the opening of *Ulysses*, and, as Hugh Kenner has pointed out in his essay on the *Portrait,* is followed by a "grim interjection parodying Greek and Hebrew necessitarianism": "In the dark land they bide, the vengeful knights of the razor. Their deadly coil they grasp: Yeah, and therein they lead to Erebus whatsoever wight hath done a deed of blood for I will on nowise suffer it even so saith the Lord." Rumbold reappears later in *Ulysses*, chiefly in the Circe episode, where he functions as executioner.

To understand more completely the function of this hangman motif, however, it is necessary to explore an additional image cluster, one that at first encounter seems to have little or no connection with it. In the Nestor episode, Stephen, quizzing his students on history, meditates: "I hear the ruin of all space, shattered glass and toppling masonry, and time one livid final flame." The phrase "shattered glass and toppling masonry" recurs in his interior monologue in the Proteus episode.

These images do not lend themselves to exact equations. Time's "livid final flame" is at once self-explanatory and inscrutable. There are greater possibilities of illumination about ruined space, shattered glass, and toppling masonry. First, we should remember that the observation first occurs in a history lesson. This reminds us of Haines' observation in the Telemachus episode that history is to blame for Ireland's plight. And history, according to Stephen, is the nightmare from which he is trying to awake. He means history in several senses here—not only human history and Irish history, but his personal history, with its heavy burdens of defeat and guilt. This motif of history is one of the many coupling the *Portrait* and *Ulysses* to *Finnegans Wake,* where history is viewed as nightmare. But more immediately, "the ruin of all space" seems to have historical connotations and to be associated particularly with Ireland, the victim of history; for Ireland is Stephen's "all space" at the moment.

To this idea of nationality we may add that of religion. The phrase "shattered glass" in his monologue associates itself with the opening page of the *Portrait:* "His father told him that story: his father looked at him through a glass: he had a hairy face." We recall the Biblical phrase "Through a glass, darkly," and we realize that the image of the shattered glass has to do with our imperfect view of God. Similarly, toppling masonry suggests falling idols, and falling idols suggest the Church or, at least in Stephen's view, the spiritual collapse and secularization of the Church.

This remarkable process of condensation presents the total image of the nooses, and the hangman waits. The stage is set for the climax, which occurs in the phantasmagorical drama of the Circe episode. Stephen's past and his tensions press in upon him unbearably. He is confronted by the apparition of his dead mother, and thus is confronted by conscience, Church, and country. To the tormented youth, it is the last straw. When she calls on him to repent, he refuses in fury, shouting again his creed. He will not serve!

THE MOTHER

(*Wrings her hands slowly, moaning desperately.*)
O Sacred Heart of Jesus, have mercy on him!
Save him from hell, O divine Sacred Heart!

STEPHEN

No! No! No! Break my spirit all of you if you can!
I'll bring you all to heel!

84

MOTHER

(*In the agony of her deathrattle.*) Have mercy on Stephen, Lord, for my sake! Inexpressible was my anguish when expiring with love, grief and agony on Mount Calvary.

STEPHEN

Nothung!

(*He lifts his ashplant high with both hands and smashes the chandelier. Time's livid final flame leaps, and, in the following darkness, ruin of all space, shattered glass and toppling masonry.*)

This violent action is Stephen's final, desperate bid for freedom from the nooses—his attempt to escape being strangled by language, nationality, and religion. It is his attempt to destroy time in the horizontal or serial sense—in short, the past—while preserving it in the vertical or psychological sense.

His accompanying ejaculation may be interpreted in several ways. Nothung is of course the name of Siegfried's sword, and thus may connote a heroic victory. Or "Nothung" may be "not hung," and this may be the announcement of Stephen's escape from the nooses. But we have encountered Joyce's irony and punning before, and we can see the similarity of "Nothung" to "nothing." This alternate reading would suggest that Stephen cannot really escape the nooses or, if he does, that it is an escape into emptiness—nothingness.

These are some of the themes, then, which are basic to both the *Portrait* and *Ulysses* and which serve to bind the two together: isolation, the Fall, the search for the father, and the struggle against the strictures of conformity, which involves the struggle of artistic creativity to express itself.

Just as themes from the *Portrait* recur in *Ulysses*, so do certain central reinforcing streams of connected imagery. Perhaps the most noteworthy of these is that pertaining to the cow. As we have seen, the image of the cow occurs at the beginning of the *Portrait*. Throughout the book the idea of the cow associates itself with country and Church. Even at the end of the *Portrait* there is a hint of the cow when Stephen invokes Dædalus, among whose mythological accomplishments was the design and construction of a clever but hollow wooden cow.

We are not surprised, therefore, to meet a milk woman in the opening episode of *Ulysses,* and to recognize the same patterns of meaning surrounding her. But in *Ulysses* Joyce explores a new area of this complex of associations by introducing an additional and richly significant motif—that of the hoof and mouth disease. We encounter this idea in Mr. Deasy's letter to the editor in the Nestor episode, in which he refers to the pestilence as the "foot and mouth" disease. And even earlier, Joyce subtly presages the introduction of this motif by significantly distorting a commonplace expression. Buck Mulligan, commenting on what he considers to be an inappropriate remark of Stephen's, says "You put your hoof in it now." Later, bearing Mr. Deasy's letter, Stephen meditates on a new title for himself: "the bullock-befriending bard."

It has been said that, since the prevalence of hoof and mouth disease was one of the predominant concerns of Dublin at the time of *Ulysses,* the use of this motif is in the best documentary naturalistic tradition.[1] But if anything emerges from a close reading of Joyce, it is the realization that almost all the images or motifs function in more than one capacity. And here, it seems to me, is clearly a case in point. The inference is plain. If Ireland is a cow, the cow is unhealthy. The nature of the disease is implicit in the dual images of hoof and mouth. "Hoof" seems to connote a state that is somewhat less than civilized, and also a condition of insensitivity; and certainly many characters in *Ulysses,* at least to Stephen, fit into either or both of these categories. "Mouth" similarly has more than one connotation. We are reminded not only of garrulity, a prevalent condition illustrated by many conversations in *Ulysses*, but of the sententious and provincial platitudinizing, centered chiefly on the past, which is displayed by many of the characters in the book. This uncreative use of language reminds us again of the net of language, and of the small boy in "Araby" who carries his chalice through the throng of foes.

Here, then, is another instance of the remarkable process of condensation whereby Joyce is able to gather up and compress a sizable complex of thought, feeling, and attitude into a central image cluster. As in the images of shattered glass and toppling masonry, so in those of the hoof and mouth disease, we are acted on by a totality, and it is a total picture that presents itself. In the hoof and mouth motif, the total picture or image seems to be that of fatuous and garrulous Dubliners standing in pubs, keening a fancied past.

Another stream of imagery observed in the *Portrait* —that of wetness—is also present in *Ulysses*. But here we begin to sense a change from the earlier work to the later. Whereas in the *Portrait* the condition of warm wetness is held to be initially desirable, we find the emphasis in *Ulysses* shifted to the other pole. Wetness is usually associated here with coldness, and this condition is customarily undesirable. The sea, epitomizing cold wetness, figures importantly in *Ulysses*, as it does in the *Portrait*, but Stephen now avoids contact with it (and, incidentally, with bathing)—and he experiences no vision of beauty in conjunction with it, as he did in the *Portrait*. In the Proteus episode of *Ulysses* Stephen meditates on many things as he walks along the shore, but his reverie, although highly complicated, is essentially joyless. At the height of these moments of intense intellectual activity, after he has composed a poem of dubious value, Stephen urinates, perhaps attempting to temper cold wetness with warm wetness. It has been suggested that urination here is the symbol of creativity.[2] What seems more apparent, however, is irony—that of the comparative puniness of this act in juxtaposition to the sea. If this is creativity, it is infantile creativity.

The sea is viewed as mother in *Ulysses,* but as a dead mother. Stephen gazes seaward in the Telemachus episode, and connects the scene with the death of his mother: "The ring of bay and skyline hald a dull green mass of liquid. A bowl of white china had stood beside her deathbed holding the green sluggish bile which she had torn up from her rotting liver by fits of loud groaning vomiting." Later, Stephen meets his younger sister Dilly, and sees in her the reincarnation of their mother. The sea again figures as an image of death:

> She is drowning. Agenbite. Save her. Agenbite. All against us. She will drown me with her, eyes and hair. Lank coils of seaweed hair around me, my heart, my soul. Salt green death.
> We.
> Agenbite of inwit. Inwit's agenbite.
> Misery! Misery!

There has been a similar shift of emphasis in another stream of imagery from the *Portrait* to *Ulysses*—that of the color green. Whereas in the *Portrait* there is a recognizable connotation of creativity involved, in *Ulysses* the color is almost invariably used pejoratively. This should not surprise us. Stephen, as has been remarked, attempts to take his creative green to Paris at the end of the *Portrait.* The flight is unsuccessful, and the connotations of greenness that remain in *Ulysses* are those of nation, decay, and death. "Snotgreen" is suggested as a suitable color for Irish poets, and this image reappears in the Proteus episode. The greenness of decayed liver and salt death may be noted in the passages about the sea quoted above.

Redness seems largely to connote in *Ulysses,* as it does substantially in the *Portrait,* external reality. By yet another of Joyce's processes of condensation, the two colors are brought together in an image of horror in the

Circe episode, as a "green crab with malignant red eyes sticks deep its grinning claws in Stephen's heart." The greenness of this apparitional goad carries with it the many associations of the nets and nooses, which work upon us and upon Stephen. The malignant red eyes remind us of the red-rimmed, horny eyes of the traditional Irish peasant whom Stephen fears at the end of the *Portrait*. Thus goaded, Stephen makes his desperate swipe at the chandelier, causing glass to shatter and masonry to topple.

The structural rhythms of *Ulysses* continue and expand those of the *Portrait*. These rhythmic patterns form themselves principally into interrupted pulsations or closely juxtaposed changes of rhythm, the chief difference between the two books being that in *Ulysses* the process seems to go much deeper. Tension-relaxation, inflation-deflation, and counterpoint are observable not only macrocosmically, in the relation of one major subdivision of the book to another, but microcosmically, within individual mental processes or moments of the various principal characters. The process here is greatly speeded up. The contrasting rhythms are so closely juxtaposed as to suggest the analogy of alternating irregular currents or the condition of oscillation. Examples of interior monologue will illustrate. Here is a moment of Stephen's morning in the Proteus episode:

> Turning, he scanned the shore south, his feet sinking again slowly in new sockets.

He faces his home:

> The cold domed room of the tower waits.

He draws an analogy between silt and time, and creates a sardonic picture of his roommates as royalty:

> Through the barbicans the shafts of light are moving ever, slowly ever as my feet are sinking, creeping duskward over the dial floor. Blue dusk, nightfall, deep blue night. In the darkness of the dome

they wait, their pushedback chairs, my obelisk valise, around a board of abandoned platters. Who to clear it?

Now he casts his English roommate in the role of usurper, with Mulligan as lackey:

He has the key. I will not sleep there when this night comes. A shut door of a silent tower entombing their blind bodies, the panthersahib and his pointer. Call: no answer. He lifted his feet up from the suck and turned back by the mole of boulders.

Thoughts of usurpation and isolation lead to thoughts of Hamlet and an identification with him:

Take all, keep all. My soul walks with me, form of forms. So in the moon's midwatches I pace the path above the rocks, in sable silvered, hearing Elsinore's tempting flood.

The sight of a dead dog, then a live one running on the beach, focuses his mind on history and the galleys of invaders beaching. The dead dog then associates itself in his mind with a man drowned several days before, and drowning becomes drowned mother:

I could not save her. Waters: bitter death: lost.

Abruptly, an incongruous, deflating, less threatening but associative image intrudes:

A woman and a man. I see her skirties. Pinned up, I bet.

The monologue continues and thickens. The capers of the dog on the beach serve as objective correlative to Stephen's thought processes. Out of the flux a poem emerges. He urinates, joining his water to that of the sea. His attention thus redirected to the sea, he meditates on the drowned man and the Shakespearean sea change. He observes clouds, and imagines lightning and Lucifer. Lunging with his ashplant, he dramatizes his resolve not to return to the tower. He remembers the hag with yellow teeth and is reminded of his own bad teeth, correlating them with the external—some shells upon the beach. Removing mucus from his nose, and thus reintroducing the earlier Irish art image and unconsciously connecting himself with it, he wonders if he has been observed:

> He turned his face over a shoulder, rere regardant. Moving through the air high spars of a three master, her sails brailed up on the crosstrees, homing, upstream, silently moving, a silent ship.

Even in this highly fragmentary abstract of Stephen's monologue, it can be seen that here is not only the thought content of the associative process but an extremely complicated contrapuntal rhythmic pattern. Each image or association carries its own rhythm, and the juxtaposition of these associations produces the pattern of intermittent or interrupted pulsations. This, although here speeded up, is essentially the method of the *Portrait*.

Less intellectualized than Stephen's, Bloom's thought processes carry their own pattern of rhythm. His morning walk gives us a glimpse into a section of his maze:

> He crossed to the bright side, avoiding the loose cellarflap of seventy five. The sun was nearing the steeple of George's church. Be a warm day I fancy. Specially in these black clothes feel it more.

Here his customary pseudo-scientific curiosity is aroused:

> Black conducts, reflects (refracts is it?) the heat.

He remembers the reason for the black suit—Dignam's funeral:

> But I couldn't go in that light suit. Make a picnic of it.

He continues his journey:

> His eyelids sank quietly often as he walked in happy warmth.

Noticing the bread wagon, he is reminded of his wife:

> Boland's bread van delivering with trays our daily but she prefers yesterday's loaves turnovers crisp crowns hot.

He soaks in the "happy warmth" of the morning:

Makes you feel young.

He considers the compass direction of morning:

Somewhere in the east: early morning: set off at dawn, travel round in front of the sun. Steal a days march on him.

Back to the pseudo-scientific:

Keep it up for ever never grow a day older technically.

Setting off on an imaginary journey, he visualizes a sentry who reminds him of his father-in-law:

Walk along a strand, strange land, come to a city gate, sentry there, old ranker too, old Tweedy's big moustache leaning on a long kind of spear.

Mind centered on the East, he roams afar:

Wander through awned streets. Turbaned faces going by. Dark caves of carpet shops, big man, Turko the terrible, seated crosslegged smoking a coiled pipe. Cries of sellers in the streets. Drink water scented with fennel, sherbet. Wander along all day. Might meet a robber or two. Well, meet him. Getting on to sundown. The shadows of the mosques along the pillars: priest with a scroll rolled up. A shiver of the trees, signal, the evening wind. I pass on. Fading gold sky. A mother watches from her doorway. She calls her children home in their dark language.

He conjures up music:

High wall: beyond strings twanged.

He quickly sketches in a backdrop that reminds him of his wife again:

Night sky moon, violet, colour of Molly's new garters.

Back to *Eine Kleine Nachtmusik:*

Strings. Listen. A girl playing one of those instruments what do you call them: dulcimers. I pass.

Then the abrupt return to reality:

Probably not a bit like it really. Kind of stuff you read: in the track of the sun.

Thus at the end we are back at the beginning: the sun.

A sampling of Bloom's reverie at Dignam's funeral is also instructive:

Mr. Kernan said with solemnity:

—*I am the resurrection and the life.* That touches a man's inmost heart.

—It does, Mr. Bloom said.

Your heart perhaps but what price the fellow in the six feet by two with his toes to the daisies? No touching that. Seat of the affections. Broken heart. A pump after all, pumping thousands of gallons of blood every day. One fine day it gets bunged up and there you are. Lots of them lying around here: lungs, hearts, livers. Old rusty pumps: damn the thing else. The resurrection and the life. Once you are dead you are dead. That last day idea. Knocking them all up out of their graves. Come forth, Lazarus! And he came fifth and lost the job. Get up! Last day! Then every fellow mousing around for his liver and his lights and the rest of his traps. Find damn all of himself that morning. Pennyweight of powder in a skull. Twelve grammes one pennyweight. Troy measure.

Molly also has her own rhythmic pattern. Lying in bed at two in the morning, Bloom asleep beside her in the fetal position, this earth mother relives the day and other days in a long, sensuous, and unpunctuated ramble down many corridors. This reverie, a gigantic and irregular ellipse, returns at the end to its subject at the beginning: Bloom. The opening lines reveal the characteristic rhythm:

Yes because he never did a thing like that before as ask to get his breakfast in bed with a couple of eggs since the *City Arms* hotel when he used to be pretending to be laid up with a sick voice doing his highness to make himself interesting to that old faggot Mrs. Riordan that he thought he had a great leg of and she never left us a farthing all for masses for herself and her soul greatest miser ever . . .

Each of the three principal characters of *Ulysses*, then, seems to have his or her unique rhythmic pattern: Stephen's complicated, erudite, chilly, and cheerless allegro; Bloom's thick, soft, guttural staccato; Molly's ample, gushing, fleshy, wavelike andante. In *Ulysses* Joyce has both extended and intensified the intermittent pulsations of the *Portrait*. In the later work he has expanded the technique both horizontally and vertically. There are the pulsations within each character's thought patterns, the contrapuntal pattern formed in the total framework of the book by the juxtapositions and interminglings of these contrasting individual patterns, and of course the obvious rhythmic changes between the overt subdivisions of the work. All these rhythms constitute further explorations of the rhythmic technique observable in the *Portrait*.

A discussion of structural rhythm in *Ulysses* inevitably leads to the consideration of stream of consciousness or interior monologue as technique. Some scholars differentiate slightly between stream of consciousness and interior monologue, but I shall use the two terms interchangeably here, because for our purpose there are no significant differences between the two. The historical development of this technique has been treated by many, and does not concern us here.[3] The story of Joyce's self-announced debt to the obscure French writer Dujardin is a familiar one. Whether he was being ironic is beside the point. If Joyce did not invent the technique, he is its definitive employer. The question thus becomes: did this technique make its first appearance in Joyce's writings in *Ulysses*, or are there earlier indications of it? We have already seen that the rhythmic patterns in interior monologue in *Ulysses* are simply extensions of what we have found in the *Portrait*, but we can go further and say that in the earlier novel we find definite anticipations of the technique itself.

To determine the nature of these anticipations, it is necessary to consider the essential components of the interior monologue. Three conditions suggest themselves. First, the perspective or orientation is internal. Second, experience is viewed as flux, which entails the countless and complicated associative processes and juxtapositions of ideas and images that are collectively described as the interior monologue. Finally, the presentation is immediate, in the first person, with an illusion of nonintervention on the part of the author.

The first two of these components are present in the *Portrait,* and the third is occasionally and momentarily realized. We have already seen that the essential change from *Stephen Hero* to the *Portrait* is in perspective, and that the orientation of the later novel is internal. If we recall that Stephen's mind is the stage upon which the dramatic action unfolds, we see that in the *Portrait* Joyce has taken the first requisite step in the direction of the stream of consciousness technique.

The introspective passages in which Stephen reacts to the sermon on hell in Chapter III demonstrate Joyce's closer approach to the technique. But he has not yet arrived at it, because here he offers descriptions of the mental process, usually in the third person, rather than the immediate presentations in the implied first person required in interior monologue. Brief but direct interjections, however, mostly in the form of prayer ("O Mary, refuge of sinners . . ."), indicate that Joyce is near the threshold.

The closest approach to the technique in this section of the novel is found in Stephen's vision of horror: "A field of stiff weeds and thistles and tufted nettle-bunches. Thick among the tufts of rank stiff growth lay battered canisters and clots and coils of solid excrement. A faint marsh light struggling upwards from all the ordure through the bristling grey green weeds."

Other instances of proximity to the technique occur in later sections of the *Portrait:* Stephen's vision of the rose, and snatches of his reverie surrounding the writing of the villanelle. But for the closest approximation of the technique to be found anywhere in the novel, we must look at the closing section of the final chapter—the diary entries. In addition to recapitulating many of the themes of the novel, these entries also function to bring Joyce to his starting point for *Ulysses* in terms of the stream of consciousness technique. Consider, for example, these selected entries:

> March 21, *night*. Free. Soul free and Fancy free. Let the dead bury the dead. Ay. And let the dead marry the dead.

> April 5. Wild spring. Scudding clouds. O life! Dark stream of swirling bogwater on which apple trees have cast down their delicate flowers. Eyes of girls among the leaves. Girl demure and romping. All fair or auburn: no dark ones. They blush better. Houp-la!

> April 16. Away! Away!
> The spell of arms and voices: the white arms of roads, their promise of close embraces and the black arms of tall ships that stand against the moon, their tale of distant nations.

These entries, intermingled as they are with factual and descriptive jottings, clearly do not constitute the equivalent of the technique as we see it in *Ulysses*. Joyce has not yet consistently achieved or maintained the illusion of nonintervention. He has not "refined himself out of existence," as he does in the later work. The flux is insufficiently undifferentiated, and the associations are too overtly directed and unified—in short, one-dimensional.

But in the *Portrait* the stream of consciousness technique is at least embryonically present. It is hinted at and briefly realized. At the end of the novel we sense that Joyce is standing on the threshold of the labyrinth, and he and we can see inside. In *Ulysses,* he has entered it.

Prolegomenous to *Ulysses,* then, the *Portrait* is more than preface. In themes, imagery, rhythms, and technique, the earlier work is the necessary and genetic antecedent of the later.

8

The "Portrait" and "Finnegans Wake"

MANY CONTINUE to regard *Finnegans Wake* as a literary freak. Others may have reservations as to Joyce's judgment in writing it. Joyce himself apparently shared these reservations.[1] Nevertheless, in several ways this final work represents the logical culmination of material initiated in the *Portrait* and developed in *Ulysses*. If the *Portrait* is the microcosm and *Ulysses* the cosmos, then *Finnegans Wake* is the macrocosm. The circle of self that is the *Portrait* and that of modern man that is *Ulysses* are both concentrically contained in the circle of human history that is *Finnegans Wake*:

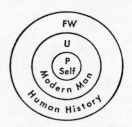

Thus, although *Finnegans Wake* is obviously more complex and is constructed on a vastly larger scale, its axis is the *Portrait* in that the earlier work delineates the individual consciousness, which in the latter becomes the archetypal consciousness. Also, the *Portrait* establishes the basic polarity between the self and the world which is part of the basic substance of *Finnegans Wake,* in which the theme of polarity is ever present.

But there are more specific connectives. I want to emphasize that what follows is merely a partial treatment of *Finnegans Wake.* We are interested here only in those things which relate *Finnegans Wake* to the *Portrait,* rather than in an extended analysis of the *Wake* itself.[2]

Central themes form one connective. In each instance we can trace a shift of emphasis or focus from the *Portrait* through *Ulysses* into *Finnegans Wake.* Consider, for example, the theme of isolation. In the *Portrait* we have been shown the artist, or would-be artist, as isolated man. In *Ulysses,* Bloom as "average" man is isolated. In *Finnegans Wake,* however, the process of universalization is carried one step further, and H. C. Earwicker, as archetypal man, is isolated man. A tavern keeper in Dublin—or as Joyce writes it in the form that emphasizes alienation, "Dyoublong"—Earwicker, embodying such patterns and myths as Adam, Humpty Dumpty, Tristan, and Finn MacCool, is a lonely man. The fading of his physical desire for his wife, Anna Livia, perhaps symbolizes his isolation from Anna Livia Plurabelle, both the river Liffey and the stream of life. Conscious of the gulf between him and his sons, Kevin and Jerry, he has become centered emotionally on his daughter, Isobel.

So Earwicker dreams, and in the dream his censorable attachment to his daughter becomes metamorphosed into the Tristan-Iseult archetype. The situation is rearranged into more acceptable form. Things come right for him. But the point to note here is that it is only in his dream that he merges with heroes and participates in archetypal patterns of experience.

Much has been made of the comic spirit of *Finnegans Wake.* I think this aspect of the book has been overemphasized, at the expense of another important strain —that of sadness. Obscured by the concentration on the comic aspect, it seems to me, is the fact that what we have here is essentially the universal human tragedy. Identification and union with mankind exist only in the unconscious mind. Only in the dream state does isolation disappear. And Earwicker, like all of us, is a solitary dreamer. As Marlow in Conrad's *Heart of Darkness* puts it, "We live, as we dream, alone." *Ulysses* has been called one of the loneliest of books. Perhaps there is one lonelier —*Finnegans Wake*.

The sadness is actually reinforced, I think, by the very devices seized upon by so many commentators as illustrations of the comic spirit in *Finnegans Wake*. The cadences and rhythms, which supposedly lend a lilt to the work, tend to have the same ultimate effect as an overly long Irish jig. They come to seem forced and laborious. William Y. Tindall has described the character of Shem as one of "painful jocularity." I wonder if this phrase may not also be ascribed to the cadences of the work. We become finally weary of the jocularity and tend to perceive more clearly the underlying pain.

This is particularly true when we analyze what is perhaps the chief literary device of the work—the pun. It is true of course that the pun is a form of wit—albeit to some the lowest form—and *Finnegans Wake* is certainly the classic demonstration of paronomasia. Yet, as every self-respecting Freudian is aware, the pun is often the surface symptom of a deep-seated unrest. It is a sally at, and last-minute diversion from, a repressed or threatening topic; it is a way of holding people off. And this is but another evidence of the universal condition of surface synthesis covering painful areas. This is the condition of every man and Everyman, and as Joyce tells us, in H. C. Earwicker, "Here Comes Everybody."

When we turn, however, to the second central theme under consideration—the Fall—we find a happier note struck by *Finnegans Wake* than by either the *Portrait* or *Ulysses*. Again, a universal chord has been sounded. As has been indicated, in the *Portrait* Stephen is not yet fallen but about to fall. He foresees the necessity of the

Fall as a prerequisite to the celebration of mortal beauty and consequent artistic creation. In *Ulysses* he has fallen, but he finds that it has been a gloomy event. The hoped-for productivity has not ensued, and Stephen's condition is only partly relieved by his eventual communion with Bloom. We are left largely to guess at the ultimate outcome. But in *Finnegans Wake* we are moving in larger circles—Viconian circles, to be exact. Here the Fall is not limited to matters of artistic creativity; it is presented as one of the great and necessary cycles of human experience. It is the "fortunate Fall," *felix culpa*—or as Joyce puts it, "O foenix culprit!" In *Finnegans Wake* the theme has not only been universalized but the emphasis has shifted to the affirmative aspect of the Fall—resurrection. The title of the book comes from the Irish-American song about Finnegan the hod carrier, supposedly dead, who, when whiskey was spilled at his wake, jumped up and joined the festivities. This pattern becomes a governing motif. Earwicker is a surrogate not only of Finnegan but of Finn MacCool, the sleeping Irish giant-hero. Whiskey becomes water—Anna Livia Plurabelle—representing life. But the "culprit" is also "foenix." This felicitous spelling puts us in touch not only with the bird who rises from its own ashes, and the park in which Earwicker committed some unnamed indecency, but with the idea of the fortunate Fall. Earwicker or Everyman, although culprit, will rise again. As Joyce says, "felixed is who culpas does."

Joyce even incorporates Finnegan's hod into the pattern. Sensing its possibilities as a symbol of the masculine principle, he postulates erection as a kind of resurrection: "Phall if you but will, rise you must: and none so soon either shall the pharce for the nunce come to setdown secular phoenish."

The Fall as motif recurs again and again throughout the work, but the following passage may serve as convenient summary of most of the implications of this theme:

> But abide Zeit's sumonserving, rise afterfall. Blue-

> blitz-bolted from there, knowing the hingeworms
> of the hallmirks of habitationlesness, buried bur-
> rowing in Gehinnon, to proliferate through all his
> Unterwealth, seam by seam, sheol om sheol, and
> revisit our Uppercrust Sideria of Utilitarios, the
> divine one, the hoarder hidden propaguting his
> plutorpolular progeniem of pots and pans and
> pokers and puns from biddenland to boughtenland,
> the spearway fore the spoorway.

Stephen's egocentric and disappointed Fall has become
an integral part of the Viconian cycle, a prerequisite
for rebirth, for the journey up from hell to the stars.

A shift of emphasis has also taken place in the idea
of the search for the father. Stephen rejects his nominal
father in the *Portrait* and searches for his spiritual father
throughout *Ulysses*. But in *Finnegans Wake* the search
for the father becomes the search *of* the father. Earwicker is searching for his daughter in one sense—and
we have seen the metamorphosis of this censorable attachment—and for his son in another sense. Shaun is
his favorite, but the Shem-Shaun polarity is indivisible,
and Shaun without Shem is an incomplete sonship. Yet
Shem and his father are apart. To what extent Earwicker
is "searching" for Anna Livia Plurabelle is indeterminate;
yet what she represents is the flow of life, and Earwicker,
growing apart from her, represents man withheld from
the stream of life. Earwicker, then, seems to be in a
state of suspension. It might be said that he is searching
for relationship, for identity, for someone or something
to be a father to. In this way he is a universalized Bloom.
But what Earwicker encounters in his search is Vico's
unrelenting cycles. It is the fate of the father to be supplanted by the son, and we as readers are made aware
of this fact by the predominance of Shem-Shaun over
Earwicker material in the later sections of the book.
Thus we are brought back to the title and three senses
of the word "wake." And Earwicker's quest—if quest
it is—is the reverse side of the coin. We are aware of

the promise of the "waking" of Earwicker, but we are also aware that we are attendants at the "wake" of Earwicker; in this sense, the word suggests both demise and a path of progress. If there is one word that characterizes this entire pattern of *Finnegans Wake*, that word is inevitability.

The struggle against conformity, so integral a part of the *Portrait* and *Ulysses*, with their respective nets and nooses, is also treated in *Finnegans Wake*. But the situation here is considerably more complicated. In the earlier works, Stephen jousts with various representatives or personifications of conformity, such as Maurice, Cranly, and Mulligan. In *Finnegans Wake*, however, conformity and nonconformity are presented as a polarity. Roughly, Shaun represents conformity and Shem nonconformity. It is "dear dogmestic Shaun" who tells the story of the Ondt and the Gracehoper, and his identity with the Ondt is unmistakable. The Gracehoper, "hoppy on akkant of his joyicity," is identifiable with Shem-Joyce. Shaun clearly stands for representative conformist Irishmen. "When lo (whish, O whish!) mesaw mestreamed as the green to the gred was flew, was flown, through deafths of durkness greengrown deeper I heard a voice, the voce of Shaun, vote of the Irish. . . ." This voice, "pure as a church mode," carries with it the nets of language, nationality, and religion against which the "pixillated doodler," Shem rebels. To Shaun, this rebellion is a form of perversion:

> . . . and him, the ciibibber like an ambitrickster, aspiring like the decan's . . . engrossing to his ganderpan what the idioglossary he invented under hicks hyssop! . . . As often as I think of that unbloody housewarmer, Shem Skrivenitch, always cutting my prhose to please his phrase, bogorror, I declare I get the jawache! Be me punting his reflection he'd begin his beogrefirght in muddyass ribalds. . . . He's weird, I tell you, and middayevil down to his vegetable soul

Thus, broadly, Shaun represents conformity and Shem nonconformity, and there is little communication between them.

Another connective between the *Portrait* and *Finnegans Wake* is the relationship between Stephen and Shem. This is a troublesome matter; Joyce keeps getting in the way. It is difficult to assess how much of Shem is Stephen and how much is Joyce. It is apparent that "Shem Skrivenitch," as Shaun calls him derogatively, and Stephen, the would-be writer, correspond in part to each other, and that this entire aspect of *Finnegans Wake* becomes more intelligible to us because of the *Portrait*. I shall discuss this matter at greater length in Chapter X.

The main connective, however, is the language of *Finnegans Wake*. Although, for the most part, it is markedly different from that of the *Portrait*, it is clearly Joyce's final assault on the same net of language that Stephen identifies in the *Portrait*. As we have seen, the net of language seems to mean, to Joyce, the uncreative use of language. Thus the language of *Finnegans Wake*, substantially a created language, represents the attempt to destroy the net.

The unit of this created language is of course the pun, or as Joyce refers to it in *Finnegans Wake*, "the name-form that whets the wits." If psychologists find unrest behind most puns, linguists find more interesting things. Joyce's puns, in some seventeen different languages, are synthesizing devices that have demonstrated brilliantly and for all time the essential oneness of language.

But there is more than linguistic unity involved. The language of *Finnegans Wake* is sacramental, ritualistic, and divinative. "He who runes may rede it on all fours," Joyce says. But this reading must not be literal if it is to be a "reding": "(Stoop) if you are abcedminded, to this claybook, what curios of signs (please stoop), in this allaphbed! Can you rede (since We and Than had it out already) its world? It is the same told of all." "Claybook," incidentally, seems a particularly felicitous appellation for *Finnegans Wake*. At once suggestive of life and death, clay is the stuff of both the funeral wake and the waking of creation. It is the substance that Joyce (and the reader) mold into the arresting design of *Finnegans Wake*. And the design is there for us to "rede" or divine, because the tale it tells is universal, "the same told of all."

This tale, which chronicles the Fall and celebrates the resurrection of man, is a ritualistic one, a compound of all myth, so that it comes as no surprise to us to find Joyce describing the language of *Finnegans Wake* as "the rite words by the rote order." For these "name-forms" are not "right" words, but are "rite" words. And this is why Joyce cautions us not to be too "abcedminded"—literal-minded—about *Finnegans Wake*. It is to be viewed as ritualistic, ceremonious, and celebrant. What it celebrates, as it ritualistically and ceremoniously synthesizes and thus re-creates the language, is creation itself.

Most clearly, *Finnegans Wake* involves much more than an assault on the net of language. Nor can it be viewed simply as a continuation of theme and polarity from the *Portrait* through *Ulysses*. In the foregoing fragmentary and oversimplified treatment I have done little more than point to the work. But to do more would not be within the province or focus of this book.

The world (or rather that relatively small part interested in Joyce) still awaits a definitive study of *Finnegans Wake*. That study may never appear; *Finnegans Wake*—dream that it is—may forever resist the imparting of all its latent content. Joyce felt that readers should spend as much time reading his works as he spent writing them, and *Finnegans Wake* took him some seventeen years. There are one or two persons who have now spent almost that much time reading it. Possibly we shall hear from them before long. I once made the mistake, in talking with one of them, of pointing out that in seventeen years one could read hundreds of books. "But they're all in the *Wake!*" he retorted. Perhaps he is right.

9

Joyce's Esthetic Theories Applied

JOYCE'S WORKS are not written, in the usual sense; rather, they are constructed. The principles upon which these constructions are based are his esthetic theories, formulated in the *Portrait* and demonstrated in all his works. Although it is Stephen rather than Joyce who proclaims them, and although, as we shall see later, there is usually considerable psychic distance between the two, here, at least, author and character speak with one voice.

The evolution of these theories, with Aristotle and Aquinas as chief antecedents, can be traced from the jottings in Joyce's Paris notebooks through their initial exposition in *Stephen Hero* to their final formulation in the *Portrait*. It is this final formulation and its application rather than the genesis of the theories that interests us here.[1]

Let us recapitulate briefly. Art, according to Stephen, is the human disposition of sensible or intelligible matter for an esthetic end, to satisfy the esthetic appetite. Improper art is kinetic, exciting feelings of desire and loathing; proper art is static, inviting contemplation. The apprehension of the esthetic object is a tripartite process: the separation, in the mind, of the object from the non-object and the consequent apprehension of wholeness; the perception of the relation of part to part, or harmony; and the final synthesis, the realization of the *quidditas* or radiance of the object. There are three forms, modes, or categories of art: the lyrical, in which the artist presents his image in immediate relation to himself; the epical, wherein he presents his image in mediate relation to himself and others; the dramatic, in which he presents his image in immediate relation to others.

There have been considerable controversy and confusion among Joyce scholars about these categories of lyric, epic, and dramatic art. The conventional view is that of the *Portrait* as lyric, *Ulysses* as epic, and *Finnegans Wake* as dramatic. Some scholars, however, categorize most of Joyce's writings as dramatic.

There are, I think, two causes for this controversy. The first of these, which has seemingly been neglected, is the ambiguity of Joyce's pronouncements themselves. The categories are based upon the possible relationships of the esthetic image to the artist and others. In his Paris notebooks Joyce calls this image *the* image. In *Stephen Hero* he calls it *his* image, and this use of the possessive pronoun is maintained in the *Portrait*. The question then arises: What image does he mean? Is it the image of the artist or the image of his creation? In the discussion of the three stages of esthetic apprehension which immediately precedes the passage in question in the *Portrait*, Joyce speaks of the "esthetic image," which would lead us to believe that his categories of art were concerned with the image of the artist's creation rather than with the image of the artist.

But immediately following this passage in the *Portrait* Joyce personalizes the concept by speaking of the artist as the "centre of emotional gravity," thus seeming to be concerned with the image of the artist himself: "The simplest epical form is seen emerging out of lyrical literature when the artist prolongs and broods upon himself as the centre of an epical event and this form progresses till the centre of emotional gravity is equidistant from the artist himself and from others."

And, in the dramatic form: "The personality of the artist, at first a cry or a cadence or a mood and then a fluid and lambent narrative, finally refines itself out of existence, impersonalizes itself, so to speak."

The second possible source of confusion or controversy in this area stems from the tendency of some Joyce scholars to insist on compartmentalizing Joyce's works and to confuse genre with attitude. The very duality of Joyce's language, as mentioned above, precludes blanket characterization. "Attitude" is the key word here. To Joyce, lyric, epic, and dramatic seem to be less genres and more states of mind. And this state of mind or attitude fluctuates. There are "interrupted pulsations" of lyric, dramatic, and epic in all Joyce's major works; and to attempt to hang any one label on any one work is dangerous. For example, the *Portrait* is conventionally regarded as a lyrical form, which according to Joyce "is in fact the simplest verbal vesture of an instant of emotion." The writer here, he says, "is more conscious of the instant of emotion than of himself as feeling emotion." But anyone mindful of the considerable amount of internal analysis and descriptions of mental processes present in the *Portrait* must certainly hesitate to place the work entirely within the lyric category. Indeed, the distancing process Joyce achieves from *Stephen Hero* to the *Portrait* about Stephen tends to place the *Portrait* nearer the "mediate relationship" between the artist and others which Joyce regards as the "simplest epical form." Our difficulty here is that we do not know precisely what Joyce considers to be "an epical event" on which the artist broods. If the development of a mind may be considered such an event, then the *Portrait* contains epic as well as lyric emphases. And if we accept the apparent paradox of objectivity achieved by interior perspective in the *Portrait,* we see at times that immediate relationship of the image to others which, according to Joyce, is the basis of the mode of drama. As has been pointed out earlier, Stephen's mind becomes the stage on which the action unfolds.

About *Ulysses*, the simplest course is to conclude that since there are many basic correspondences to the *Odyssey*, the work is epic. But in the face of Joyce's duality of definition, this becomes oversimplification indeed. If it is the esthetic image with which we are concerned, there are certainly lyrical aspects to *Ulysses*; at least Bloom and Molly are more conscious of the instant of emotion than of themselves as feeling emotion. On the other hand, if we are concerned with the artist's own image, then we cannot avoid remarking the impersonality of *Ulysses*. And this impersonality, achieved when the artist "refines himself out of existence," accords with Joyce's definition of drama. The impersonality is of course virtual rather than actual—clearly, any writer is involved in his work. But all art is essentially illusion, and it is the illusion of nonintervention or impersonality that Joyce maintains so consistently in the interior monologues of *Ulysses*.

The same situation obtains in the other works. If we judge by genre, we must consider *Chamber Music* to be "lyrical"; but if we judge by attitude, we perceive the essentially dramatic nature of the poems. When approached from the standpoint of attitude rather than genre *Stephen Hero* seems essentially lyric. *Dubliners*, depending as it does for its effect on epiphany, must, by the very nature of epiphany, be dramatic. *Exiles*, Joyce's one attempt at drama, may be called drama in genre only. Joyce does not achieve impersonality in this work. He seems heavily involved with Richard Rowan, and gives us self-dramatization rather than drama. His attitude here seems lyrical.

This leaves *Finnegans Wake*. Here again we are confronted with the duality of the esthetic image and the artist's image. If our interpretation of the work is based upon the concept of the artist's image, there seems to be no reason for not calling *Finnegans Wake* dramatic. However, if we are concerned with the esthetic image, the question then becomes: to what extent is the dreamer, Earwicker, conscious of his dream *qua* dream? And does the extent to which he is not conscious of it constitute the lyrical aspect of *Finnegans Wake?*

These questions, raised by Joyce's definitions and the tendency of some to classify by genres, evade conclusive answers. It seems clear that in the categories of lyric, dramatic, and epic, Joyce's works are not susceptible of neat compartmentation. Joyce was concerned with attitudes rather than with categories. These attitudes vary, with perhaps the dramatic predominating.

Whatever attitude is emphasized in his works, Joyce considered that the esthetic object or work of art should contain three requisite qualities: wholeness, harmony, and radiance. Since this doctrine is promulgated in final form in the *Portrait,* it is fitting to determine the extent to which the *Portrait* itself exemplifies the doctrine.

Wholeness is that quality which separates the object from the non-object. In effect this is unity, and Joyce has achieved it in the *Portrait* in several ways. First, the very title itself, *A Portrait of the Artist as a Young Man,* serves effectively to place a "frame" around the object. More fundamentally, everything in the story is oriented toward a single theme: the development of a consciousness. The symbolic action of the story takes the form of successive collisions of various forces or entities with this mind. As Stephen travels through various kinds of rejection and alienation involving home, Church, and country, wholeness or unity is apparent in that the emphasis is always on the effect of these collisions on the shaping of his consciousness. Flight is the inevitable outcome, and thus we have in effect a unified although complex picture of a mind from the stages of initial perception of reality to the point where ultimate reality, or perhaps necessity, is realized—the necessity of escape into creativity.

Finally, wholeness or unity is achieved as the mind draws a line or boundary around the novel, separating it from its "immeasurable background" of time and space—in other words, taking it out of time and space and thus perceiving it as an esthetic object: as art, not life.

The establishment of harmony in the *Portrait* is a more complex matter. Here we must come to close grips with the very structure of the novel. In other words, we must now undertake a considerably more perceptive reading of the *Portrait* than our first quick examination, in order to demonstrate that relation of part to part which Joyce called harmony. We must consider the interlocking pattern of motifs in some detail, because it is in these motifs that the relationship of part to part is most clearly in evidence.

In Chapter I all the central motifs of the novel are not only introduced but recur in concentrically enlarging contexts. We hear immediately of the moocow, which is to become a symbol for Ireland, and we learn that Stephen's father has a "hairy face." This slightly distasteful image, although suggesting a child's concept of God, is the first subtle hint of a predominant theme: the estrangement of son from father. We are presented with a fragment of a song about a red rose, which is metamorphosized by Stephen's lisping imagination into a green rose. This clash of colors, which has been discussed earlier, introduces another central and persistent theme: the conflict between Stephen's imagination and external reality. The mention of bedwetting not only sets up the connected stream of wet-dry and warm-cold imagery which runs throughout the novel, but suggests areas of misbehavior and possible punishment. Stephen's mother plays a sailor's hornpipe for a dance by Stephen and we see conformity to a ritual. Applauding this dance is Stephen's Aunt Dante, whose red and green brushes for Davitt and Parnell reinforce the color imagery and serve to identify Stephen with Parnell, a betrayed martyr. Dante, significantly enough, rewards Stephen with a sweet when he runs errands for her: a reward for conformity. But Dante is a born punisher. Stephen apparently announces his intention of marrying Eileen, a neighbor girl. His mother indicates that an apology is due, and Dante reinforces the request with the jingle about eagles pulling out eyes.

To understand Joyce's purpose here, it is important to note that Dante was not the original speaker of this jingle. In one of Joyce's epiphanies—jottings in the Paris notebooks—the incident is given in a different form:

(Bray: in the parlour of the house in Martello Terrace)

Mr. Vance—(*comes in with a stick*) . . . O, you know, he'll have to apologise, Mrs. Joyce.

Mrs. Joyce—O yes . . . Do you hear that, Jim?

Mr. Vance—Or else—if he doesn't—the eagles'll come and pull out his eyes.

Mrs. Joyce—O, but I'm sure he will apologise.

Joyce—(*under the table, to himself*)

—Pull out his eyes,
Apologise,
Apologise,
Pull out his eyes.

Apologise
Pull out his eyes,
Pull out his eyes,
Apologise.

Joyce accomplished much by the change to Dante as the speaker. Not only does this change serve to reinforce our identification of her as a punisher and pave the way for the Christmas dispute over Parnell, but it also brings to our attention the net of language—

that is, the uncreative use of language. We may be sure that the name Dante was not chosen at random. The many incorporations of motif or material from the Italian poet in Joyce's work testifies to his admiration for the author of the *Commedia* as a creative user of language. But here is Dante's namesake, Stephen's aunt, spouting verse of a highly different kind. Punishment is its theme, as it is the theme of the *Inferno*, but the level is comparatively so low as to qualify as parody. We already know, from *Stephen Hero*, the feeling of Stephen-Joyce that Dante's method as a vehicle for modern attitudes gives an effect of irony, but here we are beyond mere irony. Joyce, by so naming this fervid spokesman for conformity and authority, is thus here showing us the net of language in operation. He has achieved much by the transformation of the early epiphany. The subject matter of Aunt Dante's rhyme is of the utmost importance. Eagles pulling out eyes suggest symbolic castration, and the implication here seems clearly to be that submission to conformity and authority, enforced by the threat of such punishment, ironically carries with it artistic impotence.

Other motifs are quickly introduced. Stephen's inability to join in playground games suggests his isolation, a theme to be repeated in endless variations. A schoolboy's speculation on Stephen's name emphasizes his apartness and suggests his continuing search for identity and a father, and constitutes the first in a series of references that serve to pave the way for his final invocation of his namesake.

Stephen calls to mind sentences from a spelling book:

> Wolsey died in Leicester Abbey
> Where the abbots buried him.
> Canker is a disease of plants,
> Cancer one of animals.

This juxtaposition of dead cardinal and diseases sets up the motif of the moribund Church which is an integral pattern in the *Portrait*. Stephen's recollection of the square ditch continues the wet-dry imagery, and identifies cold-wetness with rejection and isolation. Aunt Dante is reintroduced as a storehouse of information: "She had taught him where the Mozambique Channel was and what was the longest river in America and what was the name of the highest mountain in the moon." These are of course externals; more significant here is the recording of the fact that Dante has heartburn. In one sense, Dante truly has a burning heart in her stanch advocacy of the Church. But more basically, this slight but chronic digestive disorder links her with the moribundity of the Church.

Stephen's preoccupation with language is shown in his speculation on the word "suck" and his realization of onomatopoetic possibilities of words. This motif is to recur many times throughout the novel as Stephen becomes increasingly aware of the multi-dimensional quality of language.

Color imagery reappears in a classroom contest in which the teams are designated Lancaster and York. Stephen significantly wears a white rose, not the red rose of external reality. And he wonders if somewhere in the world there could be a green rose. This playback on his childish lisp reiterates the clash between his imagination and external reality.

He has difficulty in eating bread, but manages to swallow tea. This condition, suggestive of his chronic difficulty in partaking of communion, is a motif that runs from "The Sisters" through the *Portrait* to the end of *Ulysses,* where, as William Y. Tindall has pointed out, Stephen makes his closest approach to communion with cocoa and Mr. Bloom.[2]

The red-green polarity is again in evidence as Stephen examines a map in his geography book. A playmate had colored the earth green and the clouds maroon. We recall that Dante had taught Stephen some geography, and we feel that she would have approved of this color scheme. Stephen's ideas, however, are different. He "had not told Fleming to colour them those colours, Fleming had done it himself." This is an indirect reference to Stephen's preference, which we feel would have been the opposite: green for the clouds, symbolizing imagination, and maroon for the earth, representing reality. Examining the geography book further, he comes upon his flyleaf inscription:

> Stephen Dedalus
> Class of Elements
> Clongowes Wood College
> Sallins
> County Kildare
> Ireland
> Europe
> The World
> The Universe

Tying in with the earlier speculation on his name, this list represents another attempt to establish identity and leads to a meditation on the nature of God. Fleming has written a verse on the opposite page which is richer in possibilities:

> Stephen Dedalus is my name,
> Ireland is my nation
> Clongowes is my dwellingplace
> And heaven my expectation.

The significant thing about this verse is that each of the four statements proves to be both true and untrue in Stephen's life. In one sense Stephen's name is of course Dedalus, but in a larger sense, as we shall see in a later chapter, he does not fulfill the qualifications of this fabulous name. Ireland is his nation, and he will never forget it; but he is an outcast, an exile, and will remain so. Clongowes is his dwelling place in name only; as we have already seen, he is apart from his classmates, and the entire action of the story tends to place him increasingly further apart. Heaven is his expectation; but it turns out to be not the heaven that the Church

115

advocates and has access to, but rather a secular "heaven," because Stephen is converted at the climax of the novel to mortal beauty and foresees his role in celebrating or creating it.

Stephen's mind remains fixed on the red-green polarity and its associative possibilities. He returns to an examination of the green earth and maroon clouds, and wonders with which color he should associate himself. We learn that Dante has ripped the green covering from one of her brushes and has told Stephen that Parnell was a bad man. This indication of her attitude paves the way for what is to happen at the Christmas dinner.

Stephen becomes ill and is tended by a Brother Michael. Associating his cold damp hand with the feel of a rat, Stephen is reminded of the square ditch. We are reminded that cold-wetness indicates rejection and here symbolizes the beginnings of what is to grow into a gulf between Stephen and the Church. We also recall the several suggestions of the moribund condition of the Church, and although its representative here ministers to the sick we tend to associate him with the sickness. For Stephen later, in what to him is health, rejects the Church and its priests and determines to form his own priesthood, worshipping beauty.

Stephen's delirious dream of the dead Parnell and Aunt Dante walking proudly and silently past the mourners sets the stage for the Christmas-dinner dispute. This is a familiar scene, perhaps the best known in the novel, and little additional analysis of it need be made here. Dante is in her role of avenging angel or punisher. The punishment motif is with us again as Stephen looks at the Christmas turkey and recalls that one of the priests at school calls his pandybat a turkey. Stephen in his choice of colors has previously identified himself with Parnell, and the red-green motif, usually suitable to such an occasion, now jars the reader because of previously established associations. The story of

Parnell radiates meaning around Stephen for us in that it is the story of a man who refused to conform and was punished for his refusal.

The motif of punishment, never absent for long in this section of the *Portrait*, carries over from the Christmas scene into another context. Back at school, Stephen learns that some of the boys have been caught attempting to run away. Conflicting rumors suggest their motives for escape might be the theft of money or of altar wine. Supposedly they have been detected by the smell of the stolen wine on their breaths, thus suggesting the sacramental vintage as taint and the Church as punisher. Stephen is not only appalled by the sacrilege but, an unsuccessful communicant himself, he is greatly upset at the thought of the punishment that awaits these partakers of improper communion. Clearly, the incident strikes too close to home.

Here another motif is introduced—the sound of cricket bats from the playground: "pick, pack, pock, puck: little drops of water in a fountain slowly falling in the brimming bowl." Cricket bats suggest conformity to a ritual, as did the Irish hornpipe that Stephen danced at the beginning of the story. Stephen does not participate in the game; the sound of the bats comes from a distance, and his apartness or isolation is reiterated. The image suggests additional meanings. The cricket bats will soon become the pandybats of punishment, and the drops of water impinging on the bowl suggest the impingement of youthful and unsynthesized experience on Stephen's mind. For synthesis he must await his later vision of the girl wading in the "brimming bowl" of the sea.

The focus now shifts to hands, various images of which combine into a complex but meaningful motif that is basic to the meaning of the novel. Hands can make things, and thus may be regarded as symbols of potential creativity. But it is their diversion or perhaps perversion to other functions that is significant here.

The first hands mentioned belong to Tusker Boyle, a schoolmate who spends much time paring his nails. We are later to hear of Stephen's ideal artist, withdrawn from his work, indifferently paring his nails, like the God of creation. But Boyle is no creator, and this reference to his nails suggests femininity and egocentricity. He may perhaps be an early projection of Stephen, in that he has rebelled against authority by participating in the escapade, thus projecting Stephen's inchoate revolt. His habit of paring his nails is disapproved of by the other schoolboys, who call him Lady Boyle because of it.

Stephen now thinks of Eileen's hands, like ivory, cool and white. But this vapid suggestion of romance quickly dissipates as the chief function of hands in Stephen's present world emerges. They are administrators of punishment. The sound of the cricket bat associates itself in his mind with the pandybat. He wonders how much a pandybat hurts, little realizing how soon he is to find out. He thinks of the hands of Mr. Gleeson, the man who is to flog the culprits:

> But Mr. Gleeson had round shiny cuffs and clean white wrists and fattish white hands and the nails of them were long and pointed. Perhaps he pared them too like Lady Boyle. But they were terribly long and pointed nails. So long and cruel they were though the white fattish hands were not cruel but gentle. And though he trembled with cold and fright to think of the cruel long nails and of the high whistling sound of the cane and of the chill you felt at the end of your shirt when you undressed yourself yet he felt a feeling of queer quiet pleasure inside him to think of the white fattish hands, clean and strong and gentle.

This semi-masochistic reverie, in which Mr. Gleeson's hands constitute a fusion and metamorphosis of Boyle's and Eileen's, effectively recapitulates Stephen's situation at the moment. Gleeson is an equivalent of God—

God with a pandybat. Although Stephen is fearful, it is with a kind of delicious fear. He is not yet prepared to revolt. Also, Gleeson's hands are described as feline and womanish. Gleeson is acting as a representative of Churchly authority, and the suggestions conveyed here are those of cruelty, emasculation, and impotence.

Stephen considers the rumored theft of the altar wine to be a "terrible sin," although the odor of the wine on the rector's breath at Stephen's first communion made him slightly ill. Here is another in a long series of references to his difficulty in achieving communion. Although at the moment he has not rebelled, he has great difficulty in accepting.

He cannot let the subject of sin alone. Father Arnall is annoyed in class because his pupils are unprepared. Stephen wonders whether this exasperation constitutes a priestly sin, but considers that because priests know the nature of sin they would not sin except by mistake.

The loud crack of a pandybat signals the arrival in the classroom of Father Dolan, the prefect of studies. The scene that follows brings to a climax much of the essential action of Chapter I. Stephen has broken his glasses and thus cannot read the lesson. For this he is pandied by Father Dolan, whose hands, like those of Gleeson, are soft and firm. There are several richly suggestive factors at work in this incident. Stephen broke his glasses on the cinderpath, which, as we have already seen, is an unfamiliar environment to this nonparticipant. Ironically, the eagles of conformity have plucked out his eyes. And it is Stephen's hands, potential agents of creativity, which are pandied by Father Dolan's hands, agents of conformity, authority, and punishment.

Now, egged on by his classmates, Stephen commits his first act of overt rebellion. He reports the incident to the rector, but thereby demonstrates the watered-down quality of the rebellion: he is only seeking out higher authority. He is cheered by the boys for this act, but as the chapter closes we hear the sound, again from a distance, of the cricket bat (conformity), which has been associated with the pandybat (punishment). The net still looms.

Thus, Chapter I sets forth and reiterates all the main motifs of the novel. The interweaving of these strains which has already been effected is but a microcosm to which the novel is macrocosm. Nevertheless, certain motifs predominate in Chapter I. Conformity, authority, and punishment go hand in hand. Conformity is enforced by authority and punishment, both implied and applied.

The progression from Chapter I to Chapter II is natural and organic. The key ideas of the first chapter—conformity, authority, punishment—induce the key ideas of the second—unrest and growing rebellion. Again, the various interlocking motifs carry the meaning.

We are given a further view of the life Stephen is to reject, and Stephen samples this life. His companion for a time is his great-uncle Charles, a representative Dubliner who had tried to keep peace in the bitter Christmas dispute with Aunt Dante. Charles "repairs" daily to the outhouse, where he smokes his foul-smelling pipe and sings sentimental Irish songs. The songs are ritualistic, and Joyce's comment on this aspect of the net of nationality is to place it in the context of another ritual —the alimentary. Stephen runs errands with Charles and visits the chapel with him. Charles douses Stephen's clothes and the floor of the porch with holy water. This use of the sacramental reinforces the motif introduced in Chapter I—that of Stephen's extremely tenuous relationship with the Church. As the old man prays he kneels on his red handkerchief, and we are immediately reminded of the red-green polarity and thus are not surprised to find that Stephen does not share his uncle's feelings:

Stephen knelt at his side respecting, though he

did not share, his piety. He often wondered what his granduncle prayed for so seriously. Perhaps he prayed for the souls in purgatory or for the grace of a happy death or perhaps he prayed that God might send him back a part of the big fortune he had squandered in Cork.

Stephen, his father, and Charles take Sunday walks. The net of nationality is brought more clearly into view as the two older men speak constantly "of the subjects nearer their hearts, of Irish politics, of Munster, and of the legends of their own family . . ." But Stephen's interest in their conversation stems from his preoccupation with language—another motif introduced in Chapter I: "Words which he did not understand he said over and over to himself till he had learnt them by heart: and through them he had glimpses of the real world about him." The subtlety here, however, is that Stephen, although repeating the words, does not understand them. Thus he never does come to understand, except possibly and partly at the end of *Ulysses*, what they refer to—the "real world about him." The words are "red," but Stephen's definitions are "green."

Unrest manifests itself in his reading of *The Count of Monte Cristo*. This romantic tale of an exile appeals to both his longing for the green rose and his growing sense of his own isolation or exile. One phrase sticks in his mind—the one in which Dantes (a felicitous name for Joyce's purpose) refuses grapes from Mercedes, who had in the past slighted his love. This prideful rejection, which is to become the story of Stephen's life, carries with it also the association with wine, which harks back to the supposedly stolen altar wine and reinforces the Stephen-Church motif.

The moocow from Chapter I reappears as Stephen and a playmate visit the cow pasture at Carrickmines. In the country on summer days—in other words, in a pleasant context—the cows look beautiful to Stephen, but closer examination in autumn in the cowyard at

Stradbrook reveals "foul green puddles and clots of liquid dung" and sickens Stephen's heart so that "he could not even look at the milk they yielded." Stephen's difficulty in swallowing Irish milk persists throughout the *Portrait* (and *Ulysses*) and eventually impels him to reject the entire story of the moo-cow.

The image of Mercedes recurs in his mind, and his feeling of unrest grows. He longs to meet in the real world "the unsubstantial image which his soul so constantly beheld." He is still looking for the green rose. But yellow moving vans disrupt this vision, and the family is forced to vacate. Stephen explores Dublin, the warp and woof of Joyce's writings, and the city reactivates his feeling of unrest, "which had sent him wandering in the evening from garden to garden in search of Mercedes." The context of gardens suggests that the identification of Mercedes with the green rose is a valid one.

Stephen begins to detach himself from his experience and emotions of anger and embitterment. He is beginning to strive for that impersonal aloofness which he is to announce later as requisite to creating works of art: "Yet his anger lent nothing to his vision. He chronicled with patience what he saw, detaching himself from it and testing its mortifying flavour in secret." His detachment increases. At a children's party he takes "little part in the games," as earlier he had taken little part in playground activities, but now his "silent watchful manner" has grown and he begins "to taste the joy of his loneliness."

He has become enamored of Emma Clery, and compares her to the earlier Eileen. Both of them, he realizes, had wanted him to take them in his arms, but he is strangely incapable, because neither has fulfilled his vision. It is not until the end of the *Portrait* that we learn what it is that Stephen wants to embrace—"the loveliness which has not yet come into the world." Yet he decides to compose a poem about Emma, and recalls his difficulty in writing one about Parnell the morning after the Christmas dinner. He had finally given up, and instead had scribbled the names of some classmates:

Roderick Kickham
John Lawton
Anthony MacSwiney
Simon Moonan

If the roots of the first three surnames in this list and the suggestion of simony in the last may be taken to suggest the net of nationality and religion as Stephen is beginning to see it, his difficulties in overcoming the net of language to make a poem seem understandable.

Finally, however, he "thinks" himself into confidence. Distilling what to him is the essence of a previous incident with Emma, he writes a poem about "the night and the balmy breeze and the maiden lustre of the moon" and an "undefined sorrow" in the hearts of the protagonists. From the description of this poem, perhaps the kindest thing that can be said about it is that it lacks an objective correlative; but we as readers are supplied with an objective correlative of Stephen's narcissism when, after finishing the poem, he stands gazing into his mother's mirror.

Plans are made to return Stephen to a Jesuit school. His father praises the Jesuits by saying that "those are the fellows that can get you a position" and that "they live well, I tell you." There is a kind of Chaucerian irony here, and these statements, regarded as complimentary, suggest another variation of the moribund-Church motif. Stephen's earlier pandying by Father Dolan and his conversation with the rector are discussed. We learn that the elder Dedalus has enjoyed a good laugh with Father Dolan about it. Stephen's brief moment of earlier victory is thus rendered hollow indeed. The grouping of father and Church as deriders merges two agents of rejection or alienation.

A school play provides a frame of reference within which several motifs are gathered. The play is held in the chapel, from which the Blessed Sacrament has been removed to make room for the gymnastic exhibition which is to be the first part of the program. This subordination of the sacred to the secular suggests once more the plight of the Church. Stephen characteristically takes no part in the gymnastic exhibition, but has the chief part in the play to follow, that of a farcical pedagogue. Wearying of the program, he walks out of the chapel and becomes again a spectator from a distance, full of unrest. He meets some comrades in a doorway, and one of them mentions Stephen's father: "The smile waned on Stephen's face. Any allusion made to his father by a fellow or by a master put his calm to rout in a moment." The "father with a hairy face" of Chapter I has become progressively more repulsive to his son. His comrades tease him about his feeling for Emma Clery, and one of them strikes him playfully on the leg with a cane, saying "Admit." This of course reminds us not only of the earlier pandying but of the "Apologise" theme. Stephen's reaction is significant: "He scarcely resented what had seemed to him a silly indelicateness for he knew that the adventure in his mind stood in no danger from these words: and his face mirrored his rival's false smile." Seeking a quick and appropriate way out of the situation, he jestingly begins to recite the Confiteor, and this does the trick. The boys laugh at the irreverence. What is suggested here is that Stephen, seeking to keep the inner life inviolate, has added what will be proclaimed later in the novel as the third weapon necessary to the artist. The first two—silence and exile—have already been in evidence, but Stephen here demonstrates the third— cunning.

This mock confession recalls to Stephen's mind a related incident of the past. Accused of writing heresy in one of his school essays, Stephen had evaded the charge by a quibble. The instructor had been appeased but not the class. Several members had cornered him, and the dispute over the relative poetic merits of Tennyson and Byron had occurred. Stephen had defended Byron, indifferent to charges that the romantic poet was a heretic. The cane had been used on Stephen in earnest then, and the cry again had been, "Admit." Now, standing outside the chapel, Stephen bears no malice or anger toward his tormenters; he recalls that the evening after the beating by his classmates "he had felt that some power was divesting him of that sudden woven anger as easily as a fruit is divested of its soft ripe peel." Again the growing detachment, the increasing impersonality.

He thinks of Emma sitting in the audience and of the pressure of her fingers upon his hand, awakening desire. He is now summoned to take part in the play, and obeys the summons. But his obedience is surface obedience. His inner condition is effectively portrayed in a passage which needs to be quoted in full here:

> While his mind had been pursuing its intangible phantoms and turning in irresolution from such pursuit he had heard about him the constant voices of his father and of his masters, urging him to be a gentleman above all things. These voices had now come to be hollow sounding in his ears. When the gymnasium had been opened he had heard another voice urging him to be strong and manly and healthy and when the movement towards national revival had begun to be felt in the college yet another voice had bidden him be true to his country and help to raise up her language and tradition. In the profane world, as he foresaw, a worldly voice would bid him raise up his father's fallen state by his labours and, meanwhile, the voice of his school-comrades urged him to be a decent fellow, to shield others from blame or to beg them off and to do his best to get free days for the school. And it was the din of all these hollowsounding voices that made him halt ir-

resolutely in the pursuit of phantoms. He gave them ear only for a time but he was happy only when he was far from them, beyond their call, alone or in the company of phantasmal comrades. This is a complete summary of those adverse powers which are to be later identified as the three nets of language, nationality, and religion. The voices Stephen hears are those of conformity, but to him they are "hollowsounding" voices, and he wants no part of them.

Entering the chapel to take part in the play, Stephen notices a smiling, well-dressed priest and recalls his father's remark, "You could always tell a Jesuit by the style of his clothes." He senses a likeness between his father's mind and that of the priest, thus reinforcing identification of father with Church which he has earlier recognized. He is also aware of "some desecration of the priest's office or of the vestry itself" by the loud talking and joking incident to the performance. This overt statement suggests Stephen's growing objectivity and incipient revolt.

He acts out his part in the play, but afterward he leaves quickly to "rid himself of his mummery." Here the function of the entire program at the chapel emerges. By bringing him together with family, country, and Church, it confronts him with his life and situation to date. To him it is unreal, a mummery. He escapes from it as he is later to escape from its real-life equivalent. He must be alone, and his mingled emotions of "wounded pride, fallen hope and baffled desire" are purged only by the smell of decaying vegetation and animal urine. He becomes calm, his protective coating of aloofness returns. Significantly, the odor of decaying vegetation recurs later when Stephen rejects a priestly vocation. Perhaps there is a double meaning here. On the one hand, Ireland is decayed, and such concrete evidence of the decay confirms his perception of it. On the other hand, Stephen is in both instances being converted to the mortal and secular world, in which decay is a necessary part of the cycle. Out of this decay Stephen later feels he must create beauty.

Stephen now accompanies his father on a trip to Cork, a trip into the past. Here the outlines of the net of nationality are all too clear. His father relives scenes from his youth for Stephen, but the son is indifferent and apart. His father's possessions are to be sold at auction, but Stephen's preoccupation is with his own dispossession as he feels "the world give the lie to his phantasy."

He is attracted by one of his father's songs, of which the last two stanzas are of particular interest:

> My love she's handsome,
> My love she's bonny:
> She's like good whisky
> > When it is new:
> But when 'tis old
> And growing cold
> It fades and dies like
> > The mountain dew.

This reference to dying dew offers a slightly ominous prognosis of Stephen's dewiness in *Chamber Music* and his dewy soul later in the *Portrait*.

Father and son visit Queens College, which the elder Dedalus had attended in his youth. Many of his former associates there are now dead, and the pilgrimage degenerates into a search for familiar carved initials on desks in the anatomy theater. Stephen suddenly comes upon the word "Fœtus" carved several times on one of the desks. He is at once excited and disturbed by the word. Occurring as it does in this context of death and mutability, the word suggests stillbirth and is an ominous portent of Stephen's artistic fate in Ireland. But it also recalls incipient lusts: "His monstrous reveries came thronging into his memory. They too had sprung up before him, suddenly and furiously, out of mere words." Here again is Stephen's recognition of the evocative power of language. A glimpse of a passing team of cricketers serves as a reprise on the motif of conformity-authority of Chapter I, and appropriately enough is followed by a thoroughly conformist pep-talk by his father.

Stephen is under stress. Repelled by his father's preoccupation with the past, depressed by the smothering spirits of the long dead, and loathing himself for his obsessive lusts, he catches a glimpse of the world around him: "The sunlight breaking suddenly on his sight turned the sky and clouds into a fantastic world of sombre masses with lakelike spaces of dark rosy light."

We are reminded here of Stephen's geography book in Chapter I, in which a schoolmate, Fleming, had colored the clouds maroon. Apparently Fleming was right. Maroon is the color of reality, and to the "green" Stephen this realization is enervating:

> His very brain was sick and powerless. He could scarcely interpret the letters of the signboards of the shops. By his monstrous way of life he seemed to have put himself beyond the limits of reality. Nothing moved him or spoke to him from the real world unless he heard in it an echo of the infuriated cries within him.

In other words, he is now approaching the necessary starting point from which he is later to begin forging his own reality. He has turned inward upon himself. The present interim period is a painful one, and Stephen desperately tries to establish some sort of reality through elementary self-identification: "I am Stephen Dedalus. I am walking beside my father whose name is Simon Dedalus. We are in Cork, in Ireland. Cork is a city. Our room is in the Victoria Hotel. Victoria and Stephen and Simon. Simon and Stephen and Victoria. Names." And only names remain as he thinks back over his childhood: Dante, Parnell, Clongowes. A little boy (or "fœtus") in a gray belted suit appears for a moment, then vanishes, eradicated by time.

The pilgrimage to the past in Cork drags on, but Stephen is not a part of it. Watching his father and two cronies drinking to the memory of their past, he is conscious that "an abyss of fortune or temperament" separates him from them. He feels no filial piety: "Nothing stirred within his soul but a cold and cruel and loveless lust. His childhood was dead or lost and with it his soul capable of simple joys and he was drifting amid life like the barren shell of the moon."

His feeling of unrest increases. Money from an essay prize is spent recklessly and futilely, leaving the spender spent. He clearly sees his isolation, his inability to establish contact with his family. He turns to his lusts, and broods upon them. Lusts bring wanderings—restless wanderings—in which only occasionally Mercedes and the rose garden flit through his mind. But the green rose—Mercedes—yields to the red rose—an Irish whore. He embraces her, and the soft pressure of her lips replaces the earlier pressure of Emma's fingers and the entire Eileen-Emma-Mercedes complex. Stephen has embraced sin.

Chapter III, perhaps the least complex and most straightforward of the novel, represents the entirely logical consequence of the material presented in Chapters I and II. Stephen has been confronted with the various motifs that constitute the theme of conformity-authority-punishment. His unrest, signifying incipient rebellion, has become intolerable. The dam breaks, the rebellion becomes overt. He turns to sin. And sin is the chief topic of Chapter III.

As Hugh Kenner points out, all the sins are accounted for in the opening pages of the chapter:

A fugue-like opening plays upon the Seven Deadly Sins in turn; gluttony is in the first paragraph ("Stuff it into you, his belly counselled him"), followed by lust, then sloth ("A cold lucid indifference reigned in his soul"), pride ("His pride in his own sin, his loveless awe of God, told him that

his offense was too grievous to be atoned for"),
anger ("The blundering answer stirred the embers
of his contempt for his fellows"); finally, a recapitulation fixes each term of the mortal catalogue
in a phrase . . .[3]

This is all true enough, but what seems more significant
here is that each enumerated sin constitutes a reprise
of a previously developed motif. But the reprise in
each instance is now in a different context. The emphasis is on sin, and quite appropriately each of these
attributes of Stephen's is now regarded as sin. What
was previously chronicled as a growing awareness of
self and its needs and the growing determination to
keep the inner life inviolate or at least defended by
cunning if necessary is now seen as gluttony. We have
witnessed the growing rebellion against authority, as
symbolized by the Church, in Chapter II. This, coupled
again with the awareness of self and body, now becomes
lust in Chapter III. Yet the significant thing here, it
seems to me, is that we see, hand in hand with this
lust, the spirit of detachment, almost impersonality.
We have been prepared for this by several variations
on the motif in Chapter II. Now it is in evidence again
in Chapter III as Stephen the spectator observes Stephen the participant: "Yet as he prowled in quest of
that call, his senses, stultified only by his desire, would
note keenly all that wounded or shamed them . . ."
This detachment is now also seen as sin—the sin of
sloth—the "cold lucid indifference" that reigns in his
soul. He has established a "dark peace" between body
and soul, and the "chaos in which his ardour extinguished itself" is a "cold indifferent knowledge of himself."

Pride is of course Stephen's besetting sin, and it is
one that he is destined never to overcome. But in
Chapter III his pride is not unadulterated: "A certain
pride, a certain awe, withheld him from offering to God
even one prayer at night. . . . His pride in his own

sin, his loveless awe of God, told him that his offense was too grievous to be atoned for in whole or in part by a false homage to the Allseeing and Allknowing." The "loveless awe of God" with which pride is coupled here is a carry-over of the motif of fear so abundantly played upon in Chapter I. The intellectual honesty demonstrated by his refusal to pay "false homage" will eventually emerge as Stephen's creed in Chapter V: "I will not serve that in which I no longer believe, whether it call itself my home, my fatherland or my church . . ."

Coupled with arrogance and pride is contempt for his contemporaries. A classroom question and a "blundering answer" stir "the embers of his contempt of his fellows." Upon close inspection this seemingly routine question proves to be unexpectedly rich in possibilities, and offers new evidence of Joyce's method: "Well now, Ennis, I declare you have a head and so does my stick! Do you mean to say that you are not able to tell me what a surd is?" This identification of the blundering Ennis with a stick suggests inertness, lifelessness—a condition from which Stephen is trying to escape. But the stick in the hands of the priest becomes the pandybat of Chapter I, an instrument of punishment. Stephen later attempts to supplant both these symbols with that of his ashplant—wand of creativity—in the closing sections of the *Portrait* and in *Ulysses*. Even more basic than these considerations, however, is that of the surd. By definition, a surd is that which is irrational, which cannot be expressed in rational numbers. But Stephen is to become dedicated to precisely this task—works of art are expressions of the irrational. More specifically, Stephen wishes later to embrace "the loveliness which has not yet come into the world" and to forge in the smithy of his soul "the uncreated conscience" of his race. All these missions require the expression of the irrational, and thus Stephen's contempt for Ennis becomes the contempt of the artist or would-be artist for the Philistine.

The sins listed in the opening passages of Chapter III are interrelated. Three qualities are common to all them: pride, detachment, a turning inward upon self. In this phase of Stephen's experience they are seen as sins. Later, however, they are to become in his mind species of virtue as he substitutes his own secular and esthetic creed for that of the Church.

Now he is enmeshed in sin, and only one agent of the Church gives him pause—the Blessed Virgin Mary. Here a reminder of the earlier Mercedes, the Virgin arouses the flickering embers of his former romantic fantasies. "If ever he was impelled to cast sin from him and to repent, the impulse that moved him was the wish to be her knight." But the impulsion is not strong enough. Stephen's preoccupation, in addition to sin, is now the catechism. He has the reputation among his classmates for asking keen and disconcerting questions. His concern is intellectual, and his mind is occupied with curious hair-splitting questions: "If a layman in giving baptism pour the water before saying the words is the child baptised? Is baptism with a mineral water valid?"

The impending retreat is announced, and Stephen's heart begins "slowly to fold and fade with fear like a withering flower" as a premonition of his subsequent torment seizes him. This motif is reiterated as we learn that his heart "had withered up like a flower of the desert that feels the simoom coming from afar." As we shall see, this particular imagery—the withering flower—has a further role to play in Chapter IV.

Appropriately, it is Father Arnall who preaches the sermon at the retreat. With the appearance of this visitant from the past, attendant images of Stephen's days at Clongowes come swarming back to him; significantly, the images are invariably those of isolation, sickness, and death: the swarming playground, the square ditch, the cemetery, the infirmary. The entire experience of the retreat is to prove one of regression, in the context of Stephen's artistic development, and such reminders of the past are thus suitable to the occasion. As these memories come back to him, his soul becomes again "a child's soul."

The subject matter of the sermons at the retreat is "the four last things" from the catechism: death, judgment, hell, and heaven. The boys are adjured to put away worldly ambitions and look into the state of their souls. To Stephen, the present state of his soul will not bear examining. His intellectual concern with the catechism is replaced by the devastating realization of its implications. He listens with growing horror, agony, and despair as the aged priest relentlessly hammers home his message of punishment and eternal damnation. The calamitous vision he opens up before the eyes of the horror-stricken youth assumes all the proportions of reality and reality's color—red. Even the moon, here suggesting Stephen's vestigial romantic fantasies, becomes "blood red." Brother Michael, who ministered to Stephen's illness in Chapter I, now becomes the archangel Michael, trumpeter of doom. Sin is presented as the basis for isolation, and Stephen is of course reminded of his own isolation. The tower of ivory, linked with romance and Eileen's hands in Chapter I, now becomes a "whited sepulchre."

Fear and shame haunt Stephen as he feels that every word is directed at him alone. Memories of his past appetites haunt him. He cannot aspire to the Blessed Virgin; he imagines that Emma as a substitute and he, somehow purified, receive pardon.

The sermons continue inexorably. Stephen's refusal to serve is now revealed by Father Arnall as Lucifer's creed, stemming from the sin of pride. The common denominator of the Fall temporarily links the two. The unrelenting description of hell in all its terrifying if crudely depicted aspects crumbles Stephen. A vision of goatish figures in an evil-smelling field of weeds appears to him. He vomits and determines to confess.

What he has in mind is not the mock confession he made to his companions in Chapter II.

If we were to confine ourselves to the scope of Chapter III, we would tend to accept this vision of horror as representative of Stephen's guilt and admission of it. But in such a tightly interconnected structure as the *Portrait* the larger frame of reference is always before us. In this larger context we perceive that this vision is the second one for Stephen, and associates itself with the first, which occurred in the Clongowes infirmary. The earlier vision was a result of Stephen's sickness, and there is at least the suggestion that the present one also is a product of sickness, to be supplanted by the "healthy" esthetic vision of Chapter IV. Thus we get the hint that Stephen's "conversion," now beginning, is not to be the ultimate reality for him. This possibility is strengthened by the slight tinge of irony in Stephen's meditation on his present purity after confession, as he contemplates the post-communion breakfast of white pudding. His life is to be pure now, like white pudding.

Chapters I and II have presented us with ideas of authority-conformity-punishment and with Stephen's growing estrangement and rebellion. Chapter III details his rebellion, attendant punishment, and "conversion." Chapter IV is the shortest one of the novel, and symbolizes by its brevity the transiency of this conversion. Stephen passes from devoutness through doubt to indifference, and then awakens to a new life as he undergoes a second conversion—to mortal beauty and esthetic concerns—a conversion that is to prove permanent.

The opening passages of Chapter IV tell of Stephen's devotional exercises. Each day is dedicated to some aspect of Church ritual or dogma. The interesting point here is that Stephen, now praying for souls in purgatory, assumes temporarily the condition of Uncle Charles in Chapter II, beside whom Stephen had dutifully but indifferently kneeled.

Stephen mortifies the senses that he had earlier indulged and that he is later to exalt. Significantly, he recalls the two pandyings he had received at Clongowes; although he realizes that they were unjust, he now recalls several occasions on which he had escaped punishment and he meditates on the worthiness of priests. In effect, he is here flirting with the idea of priest as father. But we can see the inevitable estrangement approaching again: "Lately some of their judgments had sounded a little childish in his ears and had made him feel a regret and pity as though he were slowly passing out of an accustomed world and were hearing its language for the last time."

In the presence of the director of the school, who is looping the window-blind cord into a hangman's knot, Stephen is questioned as to whether he has ever felt he has a vocation, a call to the priesthood. He starts to answer yes, but suddenly withholds the word. He is attracted by the director's remarks on the priesthood, but characteristically it is his pride that is attracted:

> A strong note of pride reinforcing the gravity of the priest's voice made Stephen's heart quicken in response. . . .
> A flame began to flutter again on Stephen's cheek as he heard in this proud address an echo of his own proud musings.

Pride has been denounced in Chapter III as an attribute of Lucifer. We see now that Stephen has not been purged of pride, and as he responds to it now in connection with a priestly vocation we are reminded of Thomas Becket's line in Eliot's *Murder in the Cathedral*:

> The last temptation is the greatest treason
> To do the right deed for the wrong reason.[4]

Stephen, however, becomes less and less convinced that to join the priesthood is the right act. As he imagines a life as priest, the old familiar unrest of Chapter II besets him. An instinct warns him away, and his pride now manifests itself in a different form—as a revulsion against being a part of a set pattern or organization. He asks himself, "What had become of the pride of his spirit which had always made him conceive himself as being apart in every order?" Thus pride draws him to the priesthood, and pride paves the way for his rejection of the priesthood.

The instinct to reject becomes stronger as he meditates further on the life of the priest. He mentally places the Jesuit initials after his name, but the face that accompanies the title is "an undefined face or colour of a face." The color now emerges as the one that Stephen traditionally associates with everything hostile: "The colour faded and became strong like a changing glow of pallid brick red: Was it the raw reddish glow he had so often seen on wintry mornings on the shaven gills of the priests?" With the appearance of this variety of red, Stephen's rejection of it becomes inevitable. He sees now that he will "never swing the thurible before the tabernacle as priest," and he sees now also the necessity of the Fall.

He turns toward home and, smelling the rotted cabbages of the kitchen garden, is amused that they should play a part in the winning of his soul. This odor of rotting vegetation serves to put him in touch again with one of the fundamentals of the mortal world and to soothe him much as he was soothed by similar odors in Chapter II. Priesthood has been suggested, contemplated, rejected. The conversion did not "take."

A second conversation looms. Turning restlessly seaward, Stephen repeats a treasured line to himself:

A day of dappled seaborne clouds

and wonders anew at the power of words:

The phrase and the day and the scene harmonised in a chord. Words. Was it their colours? He allowed them to glow and fade, hue after hue: sunrise gold, the russet and green of apple orchards, azure of waves, the greyfringed fleece of clouds. No, it was not their colours: it was the poise and

balance of the period itself. Did he then love the rhythmic rise and fall of words better than their associations of legend and colour?

We have already noted Stephen's preoccupation with language earlier in the novel: his recognition of the evocative power of words and the realization that it is only through language that he can perceive reality. The difference here is that Stephen's consciousness is attuned away from "suck" and "fœtus" toward the clouds and the sky. The skies are the realm of birds, and thus Stephen sees an apparition of the hawklike man flying sunward—his fabulous namesake. His throat aches to utter the cry of a hawk or eagle. This is not the punishing eagle of Chapter I who pulls out eyes, but rather the eagle of creativity. At the climactic moment of the novel, when he sees the girl standing in the water, he notes her resemblance to a sea bird.

This girl, roughly an equivalent of Eileen, Emma, Mercedes, and the Virgin Mary in one person, is in another sense none of these. She is nameless; it is for Stephen, as creator, to name her. She is the surd, and his is the task of expressing what she represents. His mission unfolds before him and fills him with wild exultation. "Heavenly God!" cries his soul "in an outburst of profane joy." This linkage of divine and mortal elements epitomizes his new and lasting conversion.

Stephen's ultimate Dantesque vision on the beach has already been discussed in Chapter III of this study. My additional concern here, however, is with the imagery of this vision: "A world, a glimmer, or a flower? Glimmering and trembling, trembling and unfolding, a breaking light, an opening flower, it spread in endless succession to itself . . ." In one sense this is Stephen's new world of mortal beauty unfolding to him. But remembering the "withered flower" of Stephen's terrorized soul in Chapter III, blasted by ideas of fear and punishment, we see that the flower has been revived (aided perhaps by Stephen's immersion in water as he wades along the beach) and that in a truer sense his vision represents his own liberated soul unfolding to receive his new world.

Stephen has undergone a second conversion in Chapter IV. In Chapter V he assumes and proclaims his priesthood in the new order. C. G. Anderson comments: "Stephen's exposition of his esthetic to Lynch in Chapter V is the intellectual climax of the novel. Stephen is here an ordained priest of art proclaiming the gospel of art." Anderson considers the three principal symbols of Chapter V to be the "Daedalus myth; the poet as God-creator, redeemer, and priest; and the betrayal crucifixion. At the opening of Chapter V Stephen has passed from baptism through ordination and is saying mass." Watery tea and crusts of bread are symbols of the eucharist; the blue and white dockets of pawn-brokers represent the communion wafers; the screeching of a mad nun ("Jesus! O Jesus! Jesus!") is a reference to Stephen as Christ.[5]

In order to render this kind of analysis more meaningful in the context of the entire novel, it is necessary to consider the reiteration in Chapter V of previously introduced motifs and to see what variations are offered here. Chapter I introduces all the governing motifs; Chapter V recapitulates them. There are shifts of emphasis in some and new contexts for others, and it is in such processes that much of the ultimate meaning of the novel is conveyed.

If the crusts of fried bread have eucharistic significance, they also serve as reminders of the past. Stephen stares into the jar containing the drippings in which they have been soaked, and is reminded of the "dark turf-coloured water of the bath at Clongowes." His past is still with him, still to be escaped. Yet the bread has been lifted from the jar, and perhaps this is a faint suggestion of Stephen's forthcoming deliverance.

His aloofness or detachment from the life around

him is now firmly established. He allows his mother to wash his ears because it gives her pleasure. And when his father inquires of a sister whether her "lazy bitch of a brother" has left, Stephen is amused at his father's "curious idea of genders." Pride is still there, and pride is wounded: "His father's whistle, his mother's mutterings, the screech of an unknown maniac were to him now so many voices offending and threatening the pride of his youth." This pride, something to be purged in Chapter III, has become something to be guarded, to be kept inviolate.

Language is still uppermost in his mind, and reality is still something to be evoked by language:

> The rain laden trees of the avenue evoked in him, as always, memories of the girls and women in the plays of Gerhart Hauptmann . . . as he passed the sloblands of Fairview he would think of the cloistral silverveined prose of Newman . . . as he walked along the North Strand Road . . . he would recall the dark humour of Guido Caval-canti and smile; that as he went by Baird's stone cutting works in Talbot Place the spirit of Ibsen would blow through him like a keen wind . . . and that passing a grimy marine dealer's shop beyond the Liffey he would repeat the song by Ben Jonson . . .

Stephen is searching for, and attempting to formulate, his dogma. Brooding on Aristotle and Aquinas, attempting to define the essence of beauty, he flounders in a "dusk of doubt and self-mistrust." This is analogous to his condition after his first conversion in Chapter IV. But whereas he was unable in the earlier instance to resolve his doubts, and eventually forsook the creed, his doubts are now "lit up at moments by the lightnings of intuition," of "so clear a splendour that in those moments the world perished about his feet as if consumed by fire."

The feeling of unrest keeps increasing. In school he

is conscious of an ever present odor of "cheerless cellar damp and decay," which is analogous to the "special odour of decay" in *Dubliners*. Cranly is introduced, and his "priestlike" face suggests to us what his ultimate role is to be—that of antagonist. Stephen is filled with impatience at those around him who worship the "sorrowful legend" of Ireland, and he is turning more and more to another legend—that of Dædalus. Hearing Davin's account of an attempted seduction by an Irish peasant woman, Stephen thinks of her soul as "batlike," and thus essentially dissimilar to the sea bird-girl he has seen on the beach in Chapter IV. He is later to recall this identification and to group all Irish thoughts and desires into the "bat" category.

The university is now regarded by him as a "jesuit house extra-territorial," and he is "walking among aliens." His unsatisfactory conversation on esthetics with one of the priests, an Englishman, strengthens this feeling: "The language in which we are speaking is his before it is mine. How different are the words *home, Christ, ale, master,* on his lips and on mine." The words selected here are of course highly functional, around which images of usurpation, displacement, and betrayal hover. This category of isolation—dispossession—already much in evidence in the *Portrait*, is here reinforced and is later to become a central theme of *Ulysses*. Stephen's apartness is further evidenced by his refusal to sign a petition for universal peace and to subscribe to Irish nationalist ideas. Here we have arrived at the logical culmination of the growing spirit of revolt we have witnessed in the earlier chapters. Stephen has turned his back on the moo-cow of Ireland.

Now the creed is promulgated. Vague unrests and inchoate aspirations find words and become dogma. The doctrine of the three nets and the prolonged discourse on esthetics are fundamental tenets. In Chapters III and IV Stephen is concerned with the catechism of the Church, but now he symbolizes his assumption of esthetic priesthood by announcing a different kind of catechism. One of the questions is particularly instructive: if a man hacking in fury at a block of wood makes an image of a cow, is that image a work of art? This wooden cow, hacked out in fury, may be taken as Stephen's view of Ireland; to him Ireland is not a work of art, but an inert, lifeless glob of matter. Then too, the fury with which it is hacked out would place it in his classification of improper art, since fury implies kinesis. But there is a larger dimension to this matter. The mythical Dædalus had contrived a hollow wooden cow, and Joyce's entire presentation of Ireland, as seen in *Dubliners*, the *Portrait*, and *Ulysses*, seems analogous. The whole matter is brought into focus by Stephen's question. The implications seem to be that the Ireland "hacked out in fury" by nationalists and Church is not a work of art but that the cunning and esthetic representation of it *is*.

Stephen now puts part of his doctrine to work in the creation of a villanelle. Here his obsession with language is most clearly in evidence. He perceives its seminal properties and views it as a symbol of "the element of mystery."

The remainder of the chapter details various processes of disengagement from family, Emma, Church, and country. The enemy has been identified; the dogma has been promulgated. Adherence to it demands withdrawal, and Stephen systematically completes the process of cutting himself loose. The sight of birds, reminding us again of Dædalus and the sea bird-girl, signals Stephen that the hour of flight is approaching; pages of trivial Irish dialogue by his contemporaries remind us and him of what it is he must escape. As priest of his own new order he now carries his replacement for the pandybat—the ashplant. Significantly, it is Cranly, representing conformity, who snatches the ashplant from Stephen, then returns it angrily. The long discussion of religion and family matters which ensues between the two is climaxed when Stephen announces the remaining tenets of his creed. He will not serve that in which he no longer believes, and he will seek to express himself in some mode of life or art, using for his defense the weapons of "silence, exile and cunning." He has come full circle. We now see the function of his detachment, apartness, and guile. These things serve to keep the inner self inviolate. As he says in *Stephen Hero*, "Isolation is the first principle of artistic economy." What were sins in Chapter III have become requisite qualities of the artist.

The final passages of the chapter, in the form of diary entries, function as a reprise not only of most of the motifs of the chapter but of many of the central ideas of the novel. Cranly—antagonist, conformist, priest-surrogate—to whom Stephen has "confessed" many of his aspirations, is seen as the "child of exhausted loins" and is cast off. Stephen's soul has escaped the restraining nets that have loomed throughout the novel. "Soul free and fancy free," he writes. Imagination and soul, to him inextricably connected, have both been liberated.

We have a final look at the Irish moo-cow, as Stephen in company with Lynch follows a "sizable hospital nurse." Stephen expresses his aversion: "Dislike it. Two lean hungry greyhounds walking after a heifer." This bovine nurse, standing for Ireland and acting as surrogate of the moo-cow of page one, is identified with sickness as Brother Michael was in Chapter I; both ministering agents, in Stephen's mind, share the sickness. Country and Church are moribund, and Stephen, in final rejection, refuses to follow the cow.

This equation of Church with infirmity carries over into Stephen's discussion of the Blessed Virgin Mary with his mother: "Handicapped by my sex and youth. To escape held up relations between Jesus and Papa against those between Mary and her son. Said religion was not a lying-in hospital." Here we are reminded of the anatomy theater in Cork and the carved word "Fœtus," carrying with it ideas of stillbirth.

Crossing St. Stephen's Green, Stephen identifies himself with St. Stephen and with the crucified Christ.

His cunning is now at work in his defense against his father's continued advocacy of conformity. "Asked me why I did not join a rowing club. I pretended to think it over."

Contrasting his position to that of Yeats, he announces his desire to embrace not the "loveliness which has long faded from the world" but that which has "not yet come into the world." This is a fitting mission for the priest of a new order. He aspires here to be God—to create new beauty, to express the surd.

Thoughts of Emma persist to the end, but at their final meeting, Stephen puts his defensive weapon of cunning to work once more:

> Asked me, was I writing poems? About whom? I asked her. This confused her more and I felt sorry and mean. Turned off that valve at once and opened the spiritual-heroic refrigerating apparatus, invented and patented in all countries by Dante Alighieri.

In the final three diary entries we are given a rapid summary not only of Stephen's condition and aspiration but, indirectly and by association, of many of the motifs of the novel. For example, the entry of April 16 is rich in suggestion:

> The spell of arms and voices: the white arms of roads, their promise of close embraces and the black arms of tall ships that stand against the moon, their tale of distant nations. They are held out to say: We are alone—come. And the voices say with them: We are your kinsmen. And the air is thick with their company as they call to me, their kinsman, making ready to go, shaking the wings of their exultant and terrible youth.

Stephen is under the "spell of arms and voices" here.

The arms are white and promise "close embraces"; we recall Eileen's white hands, symbols of romance, towers of ivory. This reaffirmation of the romantic possibilities of hands and arms is the first step in the process of redeeming them from the perverted status of punishing agents they assumed in the early chapters and from the context of the prostitute's empty and sterile embrace at the close of Chapter II. We think now of Stephen's desire to embrace the beauty that has not yet come into the world. The white arms of roads are paths of flight and creation, and the voices are the voices of creativity, of the creative use of language toward which Stephen has been consciously and unconsciously aspiring in his preoccupation with language and his fight against the "net" or uncreative use of language. The black arms of tall ships with their tale of distant nations are clearly beckoning arms of flight or escape, mysterious yet promising. The color imagery here reinforces the clarity of the vision to Stephen. Literally, it is all down in black and white. The arms and the voices are alone, as Stephen is alone—isolated. Yet they are kinsmen. Stephen recognizes his affinity with his new world. As these kinsmen call to him, they shake the "wings of their exultant and terrible youth." Wings, in addition to serving as symbols of flight, remind us again of the hawklike apparition of Dædalus and Stephen's desire to utter cries of hawk or eagle, as well as of the entire complex of bird images of the novel.

In the penultimate entry, Stephen determines to forge in the smithy of his soul the uncreated conscience of his race. Forging implies hands, and in one aspect is an act of creativity. This, then, is the final stage in the redemption of hands. No longer administrators of punishment, they are to be agents of creation.

The novel closes with the familiar invocation addressed to Dædalus. This is a prayer appropriate to the situation. The young proponent of the new religion invokes the aid of the artificer-god to whose condition he aspires. And with the prayer, the cycle is complete. The Dædalus of the final page replaces the father with the hairy face of the first page, and the Irish story of the moo-cow yields to the classical myth of the artificer.

The foregoing analysis of the structure of the *Portrait,* admittedly incomplete, should nevertheless serve to demonstrate the incredibly tightly interconnected nature of the novel. Each chapter looks both ahead and back. Of the relationship among these chapters, Hugh Kenner makes this additional observation: "As this precise analogical structure suggests, the action of each of the five chapters is really the same action. Each chapter closes with a synthesis of triumph which the next destroys." [6] But this blanket judgment seems inaccurate. Kenner, I think, goes too far here, and his earlier word "equilibrium" appears more suitable than "triumph." To consider the endings of Chapter I, II, and III as "triumphs" is to judge each part independently of the rest and to postulate upon a first reading. In the larger context of the entire novel, there is little justification for regarding Stephen's appeal to higher authority at the close of Chapter I as a real triumph. True, he is hailed by the boys for his act, but in the distance we hear the sound of the cricket bats, which have been associated with the pandybats. Thus the conformity-authority-punishment complex is still present and undefeated. At the end of Chapter II, when Stephen embraces the prostitute, we remember that this is the youth who is to announce his determination to press in his arms the loveliness which has not yet come into the world. In retrospect, the arms of the prostitute seem a poor substitute. Similarly, mindful of the transiency of Stephen's conversion and of the boy's terror-stricken condition at the time, we are not inclined to regard his confession as a victory.

Chapters IV and V do end on a note of victory, however temporary. Stephen's vision on the beach in Chapter IV remains a governing vision, and eventually leads him to his departure at the end of Chapter V. *Ulysses* of course shows that these victories are to be short-lived; there are many hints in the *Portrait* itself that they will prove to be so. Some of these hints will be discussed in the following chapter of this book.

The fundamental fact is that there is a vital relationship among the parts of the *Portrait*. Each part reinforces all the others, and is in turn reinforced by all the others. Everything functions; everything is related. This is a tightly interwoven fabric demonstrating that requisite quality of the work of art which Joyce calls harmony.

The third and final quality of the work of art—radiance—is the summation of the process of esthetic apprehension. To Joyce radiance is *quidditas,* the "whatness" of the esthetic object. This final luminosity is the demonstration that the whole is greater than the sum of its parts.

Radiance is closely bound up with epiphany and stasis. Joyce's doctrine of epiphany has been carefully studied by Irene Hendry, who considers his works to be a "tissue of epiphanies, great and small." Miss Hendry points to Joyce's use of epiphany as demonstration of the relation of principle and practice in his works, and traces three different epiphany techniques that build cumulatively to the manifestation of radiance.[7]

The theory of epiphany, stated only in *Stephen Hero,* is implied in the *Portrait*. Since distillation characterizes the process by which the later version was produced from the earlier, the indication here might be that Joyce considered epiphany to be included in stasis and radiance. The relationship might be that epiphany is a technique that produces stasis. Stasis consists of the arrested condition of the object or image, and serves to arrest the spectator. Thus stasis both invokes and prolongs radiance. In other words, stasis is the necessary condition—first of the work of art, second of the mind of the beholder—for the perception of radiance. Stasis arrests the mind and invites contemplation.

In the *Portrait* stasis is achieved at the end of each major subdivision of the novel and at those crucial points which do not coincide with chapter divisions. These successive moments of stasis produce concentrically enlarging cores of radiance from which total meanings emanate. As harmony depends on wholeness, so also radiance depends on harmony. It is the relation of parts which provides radiance at moments of arrest.

At the end of Chapter I, Stephen listens to his playmates in the distance: "In the soft grey silence he could hear the bump of the balls: and from here and from there through the quiet air the sound of the cricket bats: pick, pack, pock, puck: like drops of water in a fountain falling softly in the brimming bowl." This passage radiates meaning because it recapitulates essential relationships of the chapter, with cricket bats gathering up ideas of conformity and punishment by association with pandybats, and the fountain gathering up the connected water imagery. It also creates the necessary condition for contemplation of this radiation. At first glance this ending seems kinetic, but it may be observed that the fountain is an analogy for the sound of the bats and that the focal point is Stephen, motionless and listening. The presentation is that of motion within a framework of stasis. And stasis governs.

At the end of Chapter II Stephen's lapse from grace is dramatized by his embrace with a prostitute—a static embrace. Again, working here to produce radiance is an entire complex—ideas of hands, arms, rebellion, sin —all compacted into one summarizing and static image.

In Chapter III his transient repentance is the subject of final contemplation, and the image is an arrested one: "The ciborium had come to him." This image summarizes the essential material of the chapter, and even grammar is functional—the use of the past perfect implies the cessation of motion.

The climactic episode on the beach in Chapter IV is governed by a static image. Stephen sees a girl standing before him in midstream, "alone and still, gazing out to sea." There follows a period of kinesis as Stephen plunges with wild exultation along the strand. Weary, he lies on the beach and, in this framework of stasis, experiences the vision of the rose. At the end of the chapter, after awakening, Stephen contemplates the seashore:

> He climbed to the crest of the sandhill and gazed about him. Evening had fallen. A rim of the young moon cleft the pale waste of sky line, the rim of a silver hoop embedded in grey sand: and the tide was flowing in fast to the land with a low whisper of her waves, islanding a few last figures in distant pools.

The focal point again is a contemplative Stephen, and the final shift—from flowing tide to "a few last figures in distant pools"—emphasizes the essential stasis in which we, arrested, contemplate Stephen's awakening to mortal beauty—the essential motif of Chapter IV.

At the end of the *Portrait* Stephen invokes his mythical antecedent: "Old father, old artificer, stand me now and ever in good stead." Here the finality of invocation carries with it attendant and persisting reverberations, and comprises a condition of ultimate stasis in which total meaning radiates. The book unfolds before us, much in the manner of the rose of Stephen's vision on the beach. Successive folds of meaning open before us, and as we contemplate them we see that the "object achieves its epiphany."

It seems clear, then, that the *Portrait* amply demonstrates wholeness, harmony, and radiance. These requisite qualities are also present in the other works. Using

148

Joyce's announced categories for the stories of *Dubliners*—youth, adolescence, maturity, and public life—we perceive not only wholeness or unity but the interrelationships of the stories, or harmony, as they present various aspects of the genus Dubliner caught in the nets. And each story in turn is cohesive, a network of relationships.

In *Dubliners* radiance deserves special attention. As in the *Portrait*, it is dependent upon stasis, and stasis is clearly apparent in the endings of the stores. Joyce accomplishes this by the invariable use of a final, arresting, and persisting image or complex of thought and feeling.

The final arrested and arresting image in "The Sisters" is that of the demented priest, alone in his confession box, laughing to himself in the dark. This vision of horror gathers up the essential material of the story and presents it for prolonged contemplation at the end.

In "The Encounter" final stasis is achieved by a shift of focus in the last sentence. Terrified by the stranger, the boy summons his companion: "How my heart beat as he came running across the field to me. He ran as if to bring me aid." This is a kinetic image, but Joyce immediately changes perspective to the boy: "And I was penitent; for in my heart I had always despised him a little." This final presentation of the complex of the boy's feelings and attitudes constitutes a genuine pause. And in the presentation the meaning of the story radiates. The pattern is one of exposure to, and retreat from, an unfamiliar pattern. With retreat comes an "appreciation" of the old order—and penitence.

In "Araby" we also find a complex final presentation: "Gazing up into the darkness I saw myself as a creature driven and derided by vanity; and my eyes burned with anguish and anger." The entire meaning of the story—frustrated quest, defeated attempt at escape to the world of imagination—is summed up in this final image

149

of the boy alone in the encompassing dark. Here, motionless boy and luminous eyes produce stasis and luminosity.

In "Eveline" the final image is also one of eyes as Joyce shifts focus from the kinetic image of the young man, pleading with Eveline to accompany him, to Eveline herself: "She set her white face to him, passive, like a helpless animal. Her eyes gave him no sign of love or farewell or recognition."

In "A Little Cloud" Little Chandler's eyes, filled with tears of remorse, constitute the final image.

In "Clay" the tears that fill Joe's eyes at the end are those of sentimentality.

In all these instances the final meaning of the story rests in these eyes, and the images are uniformly static.

In "Two Gallants" the final image is inanimate, inert: "Corley halted at the first lamp and stared grimly before him. Then with a grave gesture he extended a hand towards the light and, smiling, opened it slowly to the gaze of his disciple. A small gold coin shone in the palm." The glow of the coin becomes the glow of the tale as this final static image, suggesting simony, parasitism, and prostitution, gathers up and radiates the meanings of the story.

The ending of "A Painful Case" offers a startling display of Joyce's virtuosity. The final paragraphs are a success of possible endings as the story moves through repeated intermittent arrests toward the final condition of complete stasis. The first phase of the ending is Mr. Duffy's initial reaction to the news of Mrs. Sinico's alcoholic degeneration and death. The reaction is one of self-justification:

> What an end! The whole narrative of her death revolted him and it revolted him to think that he had ever spoken to her of what he held sacred. . . . His soul's companion! . . . Just God, what an end! . . . He had no difficulty now in approving of the course he had taken.

This initial mood yields to one of uneasy self-questioning, doubt, and apprehension:

> He began to feel ill at ease. He asked himself what else could he have done. . . . How was he to blame? Now that she was gone he understood how lonely her life must have been, sitting night after night alone in that room. His life would be lonely too until he, too, died, ceased to exist, became a memory—if anyone remembered him.

Doubt now changes to self-recrimination:

> Why had he withheld life from her? Why had he sentenced her to death? He felt his moral nature falling to pieces.

Self-recrimination yields to despair:

> He gnawed the rectitude of his life, he felt that he had been outcast from life's feast.

Finally, preliminary moods subside into the ultimate one. The emergent feeling is one of supreme loneliness, of final isolation. And the stasis is absolute:

> He turned back the way he had come, the rhythm of the engine pounding in his ears. He began to doubt the reality of what memory told him. He halted under a tree and allowed the rhythm to die away. He could not feel her near him in the darkness nor her voice touch his ear. He waited for some minutes listening. He could hear nothing: the night was perfectly silent. He listened again: perfectly silent. He felt that he was alone.

In "The Dead" Joyce presents the concept of motion within stasis. Gabriel Conroy rises to speak at the dinner table:

> Meeting a row of upturned faces he raised his eyes to the chandelier. The piano was playing a waltz tune and he could hear the skirts sweeping against the drawing-room door. People, perhaps, were standing in the snow on the quay outside, gazing up at the lighted windows and listening to the

waltz music. The air was pure there. In the distance lay the park where the trees were weighted with snow. The Wellington Monument wore a gleaming cap of snow that flashed westward over the white fields of Fifteen Acres.

By this shift in perspective from the festive and kinetic scene within the house to the silent, static, snow-covered scene without, Joyce creates a structure in which the larger static dimension engulfs and incorporates the smaller kinetic one. Again in the departure scene, the chatter of the guests is contained within the larger frame of Gabriel's silence and contemplation of the shadowy figure of his wife on the stairway. At the end of the story, a similar effect is achieved by a shift of perspective in the final moment: "His soul swooned slowly as he heard the snow falling, falling faintly through the universe and faintly falling like the descent of their last end, upon all the living and the dead." Here the transition from falling snow (kinetic) to the dead (static) achieves the final arrest. The ultimate and pervading stasis that results from this final story of *Dubliners* extends backward and broadens to include all the other stories of the collection. Because of the relationship of part to part, we see that all the Dubliners presented to us fit into the category of the living dead. The final epiphany of "The Dead" is also the epiphanizing vision of *Dubliners*.

Turning to *Ulysses*, we find that Joyce has again selected a title that implies wholeness or unity. All that the title implies is present in *Ulysses*—wandering man, quest for father, search for home—and in a sense the book is the myth of modern man.

Harmony in *Ulysses* has been thoroughly explored and demonstrated by several Joyce scholars. Tindall, Kain, Levin, Gilbert, and others have clearly established the fact that each part of the book is related to every other part. With each reading of the book we become

more highly aware of the intricate and manifold inter-
connections between the various sections, each of which
serves the triple function of recapitulation, addition,
and anticipation.

Radiance depends on harmony, and is conveyed in
moments of stasis; and as in the *Portrait,* so in *Ulysses*
we find stasis achieved at the end of each major subdivision of the book. The Proteus episode, which ter-
minates the first section, closes with Stephen gazing
over his shoulder: "Moving through the air high spars
of a threemaster, her sails brailed up on the crosstrees,
homing, upstream, silently moving, a silent ship." In
this passage two factors combine to produce a total
image of essential stasis. The focus is on Stephen, "rere
regardant." The image of the ghostly ship, moving
upstream with no visible means of power, is essentially
an image of unreality. The total vision is arrested, and
arresting. And after the turmoil of the section—the
frustrations of the Telemachus and Nestor episodes
and the flux of the Proteus episode—this vision, an
esthetic image, achieves a moment of summarizing
equilibrium and peace. The suggestion here is that this
is the only kind of peace that Stephen can know or
realize—the momentary peace of the esthetic vision.
This is the meaning that radiates from the image of the
ship.

The second major section of the book ends with the
Circe episode. Here the final hallucinatory image is
that of Bloom's dead son, an image of stasis that again
achieves a moment of equilibrium after the almost
unbearable and nightmarish tensions of the episode,
and an image that radiates auras of central meaning—
fatherhood, sonship, hallucination.

Ulysses ends with Molly's interior monologue and
final affirmation. The movement of the monologue is
highly dynamic, but what impinges upon and governs
the monologue is the image of the recumbent and static
Molly. This image is the frame of reference containing

the movement. Joyce here uses one of his favorite techniques—the presentation of motion within stasis.

The condition of stasis is achieved at many other points in *Ulysses,* but perhaps most notably in the episodes that epitomize the principals of the book. We have our deepest look into Stephen in the Proteus episode. The ending of the earlier Telemachus episode contains a final arrested image and immediately juxtaposed complex of thought, feeling, and attitude which sums up the episode: "A sleek brown head, a seal's, far out on the water, round. Usurper."

The essence of Bloom is also presented to us in a moment of stasis. At the end of the episode of Lotus Eaters he foresees his condition in the bath:

> He foresaw his pale body reclined in it at full, naked, in a womb of warmth, oiled by scented melting soap, softly laved. He saw his trunk and limbs riprippled over and sustained, buoyed lightly upward, lemonyellow; his navel, bud of flesh: and saw the dark tangled curls of his bush floating, floating hair of the stream around the limp father of thousands, a languid floating flower.

Suggestions of regression, narcissism, and impotent sensuality combine to present the essential Bloom to us; with the final word comes the transmutation or distillation of his name. The stasis achieved here allows these essences to permeate our minds.

Similarly, at the end of the Lestrygonian episode we are arrested at another revelation of Bloom. After an extremely kinetic scene in which Bloom is desperately and comico-pathetically trying to avoid being seen by Blazes Boylan, the usurper of his home, he finds sanctuary at the last moment. By this abrupt halt, he remains fixed for us:

> Yes. Gate.
> Safe!

And at the end of the Nausicaa episode, after his erotic reverie about Gerty MacDowell, Bloom is again epiphanized with an age-old and static image of cuckoldry:

Cuckoo.

Cuckoo.

Cuckoo.

It should be apparent by now that the function of stasis in Joyce's works is that of inviting and inducing contemplation. When our minds are arrested by images of stasis, they are freed from the necessity of gathering new information and impressions. They are free to rove backward and forward, perceiving relationships and assimilating what has gone before. It is a process of esthetic digestion. In other words, the book is free to work on us. These reverberations that occur in, and because of, the ultimate stasis are in effect the radiance of the book, the luminosity of the meaning. The work of art is contemplated, and the emotion we experience is the esthetic emotion, wherein "the mind is arrested and raised above desire and loathing." According to Joyce, "proper" art induces this esthetic emotion, and certainly, at least according to his own theory, Joyce's works may be considered to be proper art.

Wholeness, harmony, and radiance are present throughout Joyce's works. We may postulate wholeness by saying that Joyce's total subject is the condition of modern man. This of course seems to be a hopelessly generalized and commonplace observation, but continued study and contemplation of his writings bring the realization that he falls but little short of complete coverage of this subject. As to harmony, the history of Joyce scholarship is essentially the story of a growing awareness of relationships among the works. The present study itself is an attempted demonstration of one aspect of it. Total radiance is achieved because all parts are brought to bear on each part, and it is relationship that induces radiance.

155

10

Joyce's Use of Irony

MUCH ATTENTION has been given to the comic spirit
and the irony in *Ulysses* and *Finnegans Wake*, but not
so much to what I suggest is the genesis of Joyce's
irony in the *Portrait*. Until fairly recently the ironic
overtones in the earlier work seem to have been neglected or underemphasized.

Joyce's interpreters have in the past seemed uncertain
as how to deal with his attitude toward Stephen in the
Portrait. Traditionally, they have assumed one of two
opposing stances. Some have said that Joyce took everything about his hero seriously, whereas others have
claimed that Joyce was ridiculing Stephen and nothing
Stephen says is to be taken seriously. As I think we
shall see, the truth is somewhat more complex than
either of these extremes.

The first of these positions is illustrated by the comments of Wyndham Lewis: "It would be difficult, I
think, to find a more lifeless, irritating principal figure
than the deplorable hero of the *Portrait of the Artist*
and *Ulysses*." Describing Stephen as a "frigid prig,"
Mr. Lewis continues: "The effort to show Stephan [sic]
Dedalus in a favorable, heightened light throughout,
destroys the naturalism and at the same time certainly
fails to achieve the heroic." Mr. Lewis now turns his
attention to particulars, and chides Joyce:

The *Portrait of the Artist* is an extremely carefully written book; but it is not technically swept
and tidied to the extent that is *Ulysses*. For instance, this passage from the opening of Chapter
ii. would not have remained in the later book;—

> Every morning, therefore, uncle Charles *re-
> paired* to his outhouse, but not before he had
> greased and *brushed* scrupulously his black hair,
> etc.

People *repair* to places in works of fiction of the
humblest order or in newspaper articles; and
brushed scrupulously, though harmless certainly,
is a conjunction that the fastidious eye would reject, provided it had time to exercise its function.
But elsewhere in the *Portrait of the Artist,* in the
scene on the seashore with the bird-girl, for instance, the conventional emotion calls to itself
and clothes itself with a conventional expression;
which however merely technically pruned, leaves
a taste of well-used sentiment in the mind, definitely of the cliche order.[1]

These remarks imply of course that Joyce not only
takes Stephen completely seriously, and identifies himself with his "hero," but that in his choice of words and
styles he was not acting deliberately. Taken in by
Joyce's poker face, Lewis fails to detect the joker in
Joyce's hand. With the progression of Joyce scholarship,
however, this traditional view of Joyce's attitude has
yielded to a more accurate one. In this connection,
Hugh Kenner's comments are instructive:

> But the reader insensitive to irony may still con-
> vince himself that Stephen is not Joyce simply by
> comparing the esthetic discourses in the early
> *Stephen Hero* version with the final dramatic pres-
> entation in the *Portrait*. The same Joyce wrote
> both, but, having in the interval conceived *Ulysses*,
> he drastically pruned the *Stephen Hero* text of
> several of its key doctrines, so as to leave Stephen

Dedalus unpropped against the ironic realities which were to overwhelm his soul in the epic.

Kenner seems perhaps overassured about the precise chronological relationships among *Stephen Hero,* the *Portrait,* and *Ulysses,* but his recognition of the distancing process Joyce achieved in the *Portrait* is the point here. Speaking of the *Portrait* in general, Kenner remarks: "The fit reader will be able to see that Stephen's introspective visions are constantly judged, and ironically, by the terms in which they are raised. . . . The dashing of youthful hopes is constantly hovering, like an ironic disembodied grin, over their genesis." [2]

Joyce's attitude and method in the *Portrait* are more explicitly defined by William Y. Tindall:

> Those who find a sentimental attachment in *A Portrait of the Artist* have failed to notice the tone. . . . A careful reading makes it apparent that Joyce is aloof and generally ironic in his treatment of Stephen. But Joyce's attitude is never explicit. Stephen is allowed to expose himself. Joyce limits his assistance to arraying contrasts and juxtapositions and to using a style which, following the contours of the hero's passion, becomes that passion while parodying it. [3]

The tone of the *Portrait* is substantially different from the tone of *Stephen Hero,* and a process of distancing took place between the two works. Since distancing is a necessary prerequisite of irony, we should not be surprised at the presence of irony in the *Portrait.*

That Joyce intended irony in the novel seems clear. We are familiar with his two remarks to Frank Budgen about the *Portrait*—that he had not let this young man off very lightly, and that the important words in the full title were the last four: *As a Young Man.*

Although the general nature of Joyce's tone has been recognized, there has not been a systematic analysis of the evolution of this tone within the *Portrait,* nor has there been detailed description of the specific techniques involved. And no one has suggested, so far as I am aware, that the entire ending of the *Portrait* is susceptible of reinterpretation, not only in the light of Joyce's tone but of his later revival of the subject in *Finnegans Wake.* These are projects that I shall undertake here.

Turning to the *Portrait,* we find two principal means by which Joyce sounds overtones of irony: his choice of a name for his hero, and the technique of deflation in its several aspects.

Dædalus is a multi-dimensional name. The accomplishments of this mythical genius were many and varied. In addition to his most noteworthy enterprise—the construction of the labyrinth—he fashioned the golden honeycomb and a hollow wooden cow. The fact is, in the works under consideration, that all these accomplishments are Joyce's: none of them is Stephen's. The labyrinth is not only *Ulysses,* it is the Joyce canon. The golden honeycomb is the labyrinth as a work of art. And in theme and image, there seems to be at least a rough analogy between the hollow wooden cow and Joyce's Ireland.

Stephen is clearly Icarus, not Dædalus. We are given a hint of this at the end of the *Portrait,* when Stephen, preparing for flight, invokes his "father," Dædalus. In *Ulysses,* Stephen directly identifies himself as this fallen son: "Icarus. *Pater, ait.* Seabedabbled, fallen weltering. Lapwing you are." In *Ulysses,* Buck Mulligan hammers home the incongruity of Stephen's "absurd name," but in the *Portrait* it is left to the reader to discover the absurdity, although early in the novel our attention is called to the name by a playmate's curiosity about it. "What kind of a name is that?" he asks.

We are reminded of Hamlet's comparison:

My father's brother, but no more like my father
Than I to Hercules: . . .

Hamlet as Hercules is a patent incongruity; Stephen as Dædalus is equally incongruous. What we have then, in effect, is another aspect of the father-son relationship so important to Joyce. Joyce the father (Dædalus) regards from an esthetic distance and with underlying irony the story of Joyce the son (Stephen-Icarus). By using the satire of the incongruous name, Joyce sounds an overtone of irony that reverberates wherever Stephen goes.

But Joyce does not leave it at this. By tone and technique he expands the dimension of irony in the *Portrait,* and technique prepares us for tone. Deflation is the customary device whereby he injects or reveals the ironic tone. This specialized function of the rhythmic pattern of intermittent pulsations makes its appearance fairly early. In Chapter II, as the young Stephen wants desperately to "meet in the real world the unsubstantial image which his soul so constantly beheld," he imagines this enchanted encounter taking place. "Weakness and timidity and inexperience would fall from him in that magic moment." But two yellow moving vans abruptly intrude and Stephen's house is dismantled. This deflating event confronts Stephen and us with reality, and in retrospect, his vision is revealed as feeble and ludicrous.

There is also an inherent irony in another part of this chapter, when Stephen attempts a poem about Emma Clery:

Now it seemed as if he would fail again but, by dint of brooding on the incident, he thought himself into confidence. During this process all those elements which he deemed common and insignificant fell out of the scene. There remained no trace of the tram itself nor of the trammen nor of the horses: nor did he and she appear vividly. The verses told only of the night and the balmy breeze and the maiden lustre of the moon. Some undefined sorrow was hidden in the hearts of the protagonists as they stood in silence beneath the leafless trees and when the moment of farewell had come the kiss, which had been withheld by one, was given by both. After this the letters L. D. S. were written at the foot of the page and, having hidden the book, he went into his mother's bedroom and gazed at his face for a long time in the mirror of her dressing table.

This would-be poet, who "thinks himself into confidence" to write what sounds like unusually vapid verse, turns out in the end to be a rapt Narcissus.

The ironic tone becomes more overt at the beginning of Chapter IV. Joyce is describing the effects of Stephen's "conversion":

Every morning he hallowed himself anew in the presence of some holy image or mystery. His day began with an heroic offering of its every moment of thought or action for the intentions of the sovereign pontiff and with an early mass. . . .

His daily life was laid out in devotional areas. By means of ejaculations and prayers he stored up ungrudgingly for the souls in purgatory centuries of days and quarantines and years; yet the spiritual triumph which he felt in achieving with ease so many fabulous ages of canonical penances did not wholly reward his zeal of prayer since he could never know how much temporal punishment he had remitted by way of suffrage for the agonising souls: and, fearful lest in the midst of purgatorial fire, which differed from the infernal only in that it was not everlasting, his penance might avail no more than a drop of moisture he drove his soul daily through an increasing circle of words of supererogation. . . . His life seemed to have drawn near to eternity; every thought, word and deed, every instance of consciousness could be made to revibrate radiantly in heaven: and at times his sense of such immediate repercussion was so lively that he seemed to feel his soul in devotion pressing like fingers the keyboard of a great cash register and to see the amount of his purchase start forth immediately in heaven, not as a number but as a frail column of incense or as a slender flower.

Here, the effect of such ideas as Stephen's neat devotional compartmentation, his heroic ejaculatory mitigation of the plight of multitudes in purgatory, and his dutiful soul driving prepare for the central and inclusive idea—the incense-producing cash register—clearly an image of irony. And his ensuing attempts at self-mortification are infused with satiric overtones that reverberate when Stephen, forcing himself to smell stale odors, says: "I have amended my life, have I not?"

Further deflations await Joyce's hero. The contrapuntal pattern of the scene on the beach has already been mentioned. This juxtaposition of earthbound and unfeeling banter with Stephen's lyric attempt to soar serves as an agent not only of alienation but of deflation, and Stephen's attitudes are thus made to seem slightly ridiculous in context. Later, the pronounced deflation that jerks him back from the contemplation of his vision to the realities of watery tea and crusts of fried bread serves to orient the entire incident within a frame of irony.

Alienation and deflation go hand in hand most devastatingly in the scene in which Stephen expounds his esthetic theories to Lynch. The comments of this irreverent audience of one—his hangover, Venus' backside, and cowdung—serve as agents of both alienation and deflation. At every turn throughout the discourse his mundane applications of Stephen's theories serve to point a finger of ridicule at them. Art to Stephen is the human disposition of sensible or intelligible matter for an esthetic end. But the only esthetic end desired by Lynch is a job paying five hundred a year. Stephen illustrates one of his points by reference to the hypothenuse of a right-angled triangle, but Lynch prefers the hypothenuse of the Venus of Praxiteles. Stephen tries

to illustrate another point, and searches for an example:
"—Let us take woman—said Stephen.

"—Let us take her!—said Lynch fervently." But
Lynch is not the only agent of deflation: "A long dray
laden with old iron came round the corner of Sir Patrick
Dun's hospital covering the end of Stephen's speech
with the harsh roar of jangled and rattling metal." Stephen persists, however. He postulates his three qualities
of the esthetic object and wins mock applause from
Lynch: "—Bull's eye again!—said Lynch wittily. Tell
me now what is claritas and you win the cigar.—" Stephen does so, enamored of his theories: "Stephen paused
and, though his companion did not speak, felt that his
words had called up around them a thought enchanted
silence." But the enchantment of silence fades when
Stephen tries out his esthetic catechism on Lynch:

—*If a man hacking in fury at a block of wood*—
Stephen continued—*make there an image of a
cow, is that image a work of art? If not, why not?*—
—That's a lovely one—said Lynch, laughing
again.—That has the true scholastic stink.— [4]

Stephen now reaches the climax of his discourse, and
approaches what may be his key doctrine—that of the
impersonality of the artist: "The artist, like the God of
the creation, remains within or behind or beyond or
above his handiwork, invisible, refined out of existence,
indifferent, paring his fingernails." But his companion,
true to form, counters with this *reductio ad absurdum:*
"—Trying to refine them also out of existence—said
Lynch." Rain begins to fall, and the two seek shelter.
And with the rain comes the final deflation: "—What
do you mean—Lynch asked surlily—by prating about
beauty and the imagination in this miserable God for-
saken island? No wonder the artist retired within or behind his handiwork after having perpetrated this country.—" This final observation, which effectively throws
cold water on all Stephen's discourse, ends the scene.
Stephen's theories have been buffeted by Lynch, epit-

163

omizing external reality, and, thus buffeted, emerge into the open air having lost some of the glitter that was theirs while safely ensconced in the cloister of Stephen's mind.

If Stephen's esthetic theory is treated at least part ironically, so is his artistic production. The process of composition of the villanelle is described lyrically enough, but the context is onanistic; the framework of the scene is thus one of irony.

A further deflation, one of the most powerful in the *Portrait*, awaits Stephen in the final chapter, as he drifts into erotic reverie:

> It was not thought nor vision, though he knew vaguely that her figure was passing homeward through the city. Vaguely first and then more sharply he smelt her body. A conscious unrest seethed in his blood. Yes, it was her body he smelt: a wild and languid smell: the tepid limbs over which his music had flowed desirously and the secret soft linen upon which her flesh distilled odour and a dew.
>
> A louse crawled over the nape of his neck and, putting his thumb and forefinger deftly beneath his loose collar, he caught it.

If the flesh of his beloved distills "odour and a dew," Stephen's flesh distills a louse. This abrupt and jarring juxtaposition effectively deflates his throbbing vision.

In the diary entries that constitute the final section of the *Portrait* we find Stephen posing as martyr: "Crossing Stephen's, that is, my green . . ." This self-identification with the historical martyr gives us another of Joyce's controlled glimpses of Stephen; by the use of this association, Joyce gives us a carefully balanced view in which judgment and sympathy go hand in hand. There is considerable truth in Stephen's equation of alienation with martyrdom, and there is also more than a grain of irony.

This brings us to the ending of the *Portrait,* and to Stephen's proclamation: "Welcome, O life! I go to encounter for the millionth time the reality of experience and to forge in the smithy of my soul the uncreated conscience of my race." Stephen is completely serious in making this statement, but I suggest that our reaction to it becomes inevitably a mixed one and that there are several reasons for this.

First, we are aware that this is quite a heroic attitude Stephen is striking here, and in retrospect we cannot avoid sensing that Joyce's tone is slightly ironic. Stephen is going to encounter "for the millionth time the reality of experience," but we are aware that his encounters with the reality of experience in the past have usually led to his rejection of that reality.

Stephen in essence is playing God, and will forge the "uncreated conscience" of his race. Whether we interpret the word "conscience" as having to do with morality or whether we are mindful of its derivation from a word meaning "consciousness"—and readers of Joyce become aware that most of his key words are used in more than one sense—the implication is the same. Stephen is here postulating himself as supreme creator.

But the key word in the entire passage, it seems to me, is the verb "forge." One meaning is explicit: to create. But to grasp another possibility, it is necessary at this point to reconsider the relationship between the *Portrait* and *Finnegans Wake.* I refer particularly to the Stephen-Shem correspondence and those aspects of Shem which have particular relevance to the ending of the *Portrait.*

Shem is described in Chapter VII of *Finnegans Wake* as "that greekenhearted yude." The identification is clear. Dedalus is a Greek name, "yude" suggests both "youth" and "Jew," and "Jew" suggests "exile." The idea of exile is further developed: "He even ran away with himself and became a farsoonerite, saying he would far sooner muddle through the hash of lentils in Europe than meddle with Irrland's split little pea." This reference to European lentils and "Irrland's" (errorland's) split little pea acts as further connective to the plate of lentils in "The Two Gallants" and the gesture Stephen makes at the end of the *Portrait*, "like a fellow throwing a handful of peas up into the air."

The ship on which "the as yet unremuneranded national apostate" takes flight is suitably named: *Pridewin*. But pride does not prevent him from gleaning the words of others: "All the time he kept on treasuring with condign satisfaction each and every crumb of trektalk, covetous of his neighbor's word. . . ." Gleaner now becomes thief and forger: "what do you think Vulgariano did but study with stolen fruit how cutely to copy all their various styles of signature so as one day to utter an epical forged cheque on the public for his own private profit." But the "epical cheque" is not the only forgery: "Who can say how many pseudostylic shamiana, how few or how many of the most venerated public impostures, how very many piously forged palimpsests slipped in the first place by this morbid process from his pelagiarist pen?" This forger "used to stipple endlessly inartistic portraits of himself" which may be defined as "messes of mottage." This latter felicitous phrase again reinforces the motifs of lentils and birthrights. In short, this forger "winged away on a wildgoup's chase across the kathartic ocean and made synthetic ink and sensitive paper for his own end out of his wit's waste." And later, Shaun accuses Shem of "wordsharping." This coinage suggests cheating with words or counterfeiting them.

The picture is clear. Shem the Penman is a forger, and it does not surprise us to find him connected with "Makefearsome's Ocean," Joyce's equivalent for the famous literary forgery.

Critics disagree about Joyce's attitude toward Shem and the extent of his detachment. Some consider that he is considerably more objective in his treatment of Shem than of Stephen. Others, however, find him deeply and somewhat painfully involved with Shem. I incline toward this latter view. It seems evident from the passages quoted above that much of the material about Shem applies more directly to Joyce himself than it does to Stephen. If the "epical forged cheque" refers to *Ulysses,* it was Joyce who wrote it. And Shem, the man who flew across the "kathartic" ocean sounds suspiciously like Joyce, who in his poem "The Holy Office" wrote:

> Myself unto myself will give
> This name, Katharsis—Purgative.

The extent of Joyce's involvement with Shem is of course problematical, but the portrait of Shem does seem to be done with a rather heavy hand. It is not impossible that Joyce was being deliberately heavy-handed to emphasize the ironic connotations of the ending of the *Portrait.* And here we return to the word "forge."

According to Eugene Jolas, Joyce "was always astonished that so few people had commented on the comic spirit in his writings." [5] And if there were few general comments of this nature during his lifetime, there were none directed at this aspect of the *Portrait.* Even after his death, no one seems to have commented specifically upon the ironic overtones of the word "forge" at the ending of the novel.[6]

The idea of Stephen as forger should not surprise us. His pitifully few attempts at artistic creation in the *Portrait* are narcissistic or onanistic forgeries. Whether out of bitterness or because of a desire to reveal and emphasize, Joyce gives us a portrait of Shem as a caricature of Stephen. This later glimpse confirms or exposes the generally overlooked ironic implications of the ending of the *Portrait. Ulysses* is the intermediate step. "Signatures of all things I am here to read," meditates Stephen in the Proteus episode. But an artist is here neither to read signatures nor to forge them, but to originate them.

Thus, the irony of the ending of the *Portrait* is dramatic irony. Stephen intends one meaning, but we are conscious not only of his meaning but of another. We view him as a youth assuming a mission for which he is not yet qualified.

I have not intended to imply that the *Portrait* is out and out satire: it is not. "Irony" is the more accurate word, and irony is only one of the several aspects or dimensions of this novel. Joyce's ironic tone is not constantly present; it is used occasionally, but always with telling effect. When present, it constitutes a surrounding aura through which we view Stephen. And this aura, ironically, does not obscure him—it reveals him. It is most overtly in evidence in connection with two aspects of Stephen's life: his temporary conversion, and his attitudes toward art and the artist. And here, I think, we arrive at a distinction. It is not Stephen's actions that are customarily viewed ironically, it is his attitudes. When he is deflated, it is by his own terms, and the deflations come when his attitudes are confronted by external realities.

I am aware that to establish the presence of irony in the *Portrait* is to raise serious questions, and here I must deal with the second of the opposing critical stances mentioned at the beginning of this chapter. If Stephen is an object of irony, can he be taken seriously as a vehicle for the criticism of those aspects of Ireland seemingly under fire in Joyce's novel? And what of Stephen's aspiration to "forge . . . the uncreated conscience" of his race—is Joyce ridiculing this aspiration? Is he sneering at the moral purpose seemingly implied in the statement? I believe that the answer to the first question is yes, to the others, no.

Several observations may be made here, the combined import of which supplies these answers. In the first place, we must always remember Joyce's distinction between proper and improper art. Proper art is above and beyond desire or loathing; it is subject matter for contemplation. In writing the *Portrait*, Joyce was not writing a tract. He was directing his novel at readers of mature imagination, capable of absorbing the multidimensional meaning of the structure, of which irony is one dimension.

Second, much of the irony in the novel manifests itself in the repeated clashes between Stephen's artistic imagination and the world of external reality. Surely the implication here is that the world in which Stephen finds himself submerged—the world he is trying to escape—is no fertile breeding ground for art or creative endeavor. Thus the "criticism" of Church and country to be found in the *Portrait*—mainly in the form of suggestion, image, rhythm, and tone—can, I think, be taken seriously.

To repeat an earlier observation, it is Stephen's attitudes that are presented ironically, rather than the ideas he is promulgating. We have seen that his ideas on art and esthetic theory were certainly taken seriously by Joyce, who constructed his works upon them. But here is Stephen glibly announcing dogma. The natural question is: Why is he not creating instead of codifying? The few scraps of verse we may credit him with in the course of the *Portrait* hardly qualify him as an authority. He seems more concerned with himself and his self-announced mission at the moment than he does with real creativity.

We arrive now at the question of the "uncreated conscience." The irony here is not directed at the idea itself but at the fact that Stephen is as yet in no position to forge it except in the pejorative sense. We must remind ourselves again of the esthetic distance separating Joyce from Stephen. As is clearly evident from reading his works, Joyce passed through and emerged from the "Stephen" phase and, by the very writing of his works, forged the uncreated conscience of his race. No writer who was so keenly aware of spiritual hungers, who so consistently wrote against sham, pretense, hypocrisy, insensitivity, and unthinking conformity, who upheld integrity and honesty was, to say the very least, insensitive to moral considerations. We may quite safely conclude, I think, that the forging of the uncreated conscience was a legitimate and vital mission to Joyce, and one not to be ridiculed. And if there is irony in Stephen's announcement, it is the irony of a young esthete who, before he is qualified to undertake such a task, has much yet to learn and does not realize it.

Finally, it is helpful to remember, at the risk of reiteration, that irony is not everywhere and at all times present in the novel. I have described many of Joyce's techniques and rhythms as being patterns of interrupted or intermittent pulsations, and his tone in the *Portrait*, I think, constitutes another such pattern. Joyce coins a word in *Ulysses* which seems to fit here. That word is "jocoserious." As we consider the *Portrait*, with its fluctuations of tone pattern, we realize that it is a "jocoserious" novel. Realizing this, we are in a position to see that the comic spirit in Joyce's later writings, now generally recognized, did not originate in a vacuum, and that the seeds of it can be seen in the *Portrait*.

11

Joyce's Visual Imagination

As the thoughtful reader examines the *Portrait* he becomes increasingly aware of the extent to which Joyce relies on the visual to achieve his effects. Nearly all the central images of the novel are visual. Such an observation is, however, at odds with the traditional and established view of the nature of Joyce's imagination and raises the question, Is this reliance on the visual peculiar to the *Portrait?* To deal with this problem adequately we must go well beyond the *Portrait* in the Joyce canon—and rightfully so—because if the *Portrait* may be regarded as a kind of handbook to the other writings, we should expect that what is true of the *Portrait* in this connection is true of the other works as well. As I shall attempt to show, this is the case. But first we must examine the traditional view of Joyce's imagination.

"Ineluctable modality of the visible," muses Stephen Dedalus on the beach in the Proteus episode of *Ulysses*, "at least that if no more. Thought through my eyes." If Joyce is willing to grant the inevitability of this modality to Stephen, scholars and critics seem strangely reluctant to grant it to Joyce.

Apparently adopting as a premise Joyce's poor eyesight, they have dwelt upon the auditory aspects of his writing and imagination almost to the exclusion of the visual. T. S. Eliot has observed that Joyce wrote primarily for the ear and that he was in this sense analogous to Milton. Harry Levin has characterized Joyce's writing as being of "low visibility," his imagination as being auditory rather than visual, and his most direct concern being with the ear rather than the eye. Levin has also supported the Joyce-Milton analogy. And Richard Kain has commented that *Ulysses* describes a world of sound.[1]

No one would deny that Joyce had poor eyesight, keen ears, was preoccupied with language, and frequently used musical forms and effects in his writing. But the premise that poor eyesight inevitably results in writing strong in auditory imagery and weak in visual imagery does not prove itself. The impairment of one sense does not necessarily result in a diminished artistic representation of that sense. Beethoven is an obvious example, and Milton is even more germane. Interestingly enough, recent Milton scholarship seems to indicate that even after his blindness his imagery remained primarily visual. Thus, ironically, the analogy between Joyce and Milton, though a legitimate one, means the opposite of what Eliot and Levin apparently intended.

The demonstrable fact is that Joyce was thoroughly at home with the visual, and relied on it to achieve some of his most telling and important effects. In the *Portrait* we have on the one hand the images clustering around the conformity-authority-punishment axis—the moo-cow, eagles pulling out eyes, the pandybat. Then there are the images that represent the wooing and winning of Stephen to a life of artistic creativity—the intricate pattern of hand-and-arm imagery, the apparition of the hawklike man flying sunward over the sea, the girl on the beach, and Stephen's vision of the unfolding flower. This is only a brief listing of the motifs or images that address themselves directly to the eye. Clearly, they indicate a visual imagination on the part of their creator. The failure to appreciate this fact inevitably robs the reader, and results in an unbalanced or one-dimensional view of Joyce.

In a sense, Joyce himself is partly responsible for this unbalanced view of the nature of his imagination. It is well known that in *Finnegans Wake* he identifies himself with the ear rather than with the eye and, as a corollary, with time rather than with space. Shaun and Shem have many surrogates: the Mookse and the Gripes, the Ondt and the Gracehoper, Jute and Mutt, and Chuff and Glugg—to name some of the best-known. In each instance Shem, posing variously as the Gripes, the Gracehoper, Mutt, and Glugg, identifies himself with the ear and time. As Mutt, he proclaims himself an "utterer" and is advised by Jute to become "a bit-skin more wiseable." As Glugg, he defends time against Chuff's space. As the Gripes, "He was much to schystimatically auricular about his ens" and he "could but ill see." And as the Gracehoper, he is "blind as a batflea."

It is safe to say that Shem and his surrogates stand as approximations of Joyce, and that this identification of Shem with the ear suggests a self-identification by Joyce. Such an identification would be a natural one here. *Finnegans Wake* was written during a period when Joyce's eyesight was poor indeed, and in this work he was more directly concerned with language as language than in his earlier works.

This self-identification comes under the heading of "intention"; and if intention constitutes one kind of evidence, I suggest that a more relevant body of evidence may be found in Joyce's texts themselves. And this evidence, as I shall attempt to show, indicates that Joyce as a writer is completely at home in the visual and uses visual techniques extensively in his writings. We find them not only in the *Portrait* but in *Dubliners*, *Ulysses*, and *Finnegans Wake* as well.

In discussing Joyce's use of the visual, it is necessary

by way of preface to consider his relationship to the motion picture. In 1902 when he first went to Paris the cinema was in a more advanced stage of development than is generally realized. The motion pictures of Georges Méliès, the first great craftsman of this new art form, were being shown to large crowds. By 1900 this former magician had made more than two hundred of what he described as "magical, mystical, and trick films," each lasting one or two minutes. Méliès incorporated many new and startling effects into his pictures. He was probably the first to use certain devices now standard in motion pictures—fade-ins, dissolves, and double exposures or superimpositions—all of which devices helped to create what he described as "artificially arranged scenes," thus taking his motion pictures out of the category of straight photographic reportage. That his productions at the turn of the century were imaginative in concept and character is shown by such titles as *Cinderella, The Christmas Dream,* and *The Seven Deadly Sins.*

Méliès steadily increased his output. In 1903 and 1904 he copyrighted some sixty-four films in the United States. Since it was the normal procedure to show these films in France before exporting them, it seems reasonable to assume that they were available and being shown in Paris in 1902.

During Joyce's first sojourn in Paris, he stayed at the Grand Hôtel Corneille in the Rue Corneille, a distance of perhaps two miles from the Théâtre Robert Houdin, where the films were being shown. In the absence of positive evidence, it is of course idle to speculate on whether the young Joyce saw any of Méliès' motion pictures during his first or second stay in Paris, or if he did, whether they exerted any direct influence on his writing. But the fact remains that at some time before the year 1909 Joyce had become deeply interested in motion pictures, because in that year he persuaded four Austrian businessmen to back him financially in an attempt to establish motion picture theaters in Ireland.

Joyce returned to Dublin in October, 1909, found a promising site, and began the construction of the Volta Theatre. This theater opened Christmas week with a program of Italian films. Although business was apparently good, Joyce returned to Trieste the following month for reasons of health and domestic concerns. One of his associates in the venture continued to operate the theater for five months, but then lost heart and, over the protests of Joyce, sold the theater to an English company. Joyce is said to have received one thousand crowns as his share of the partnership.[2]

The second known association of Joyce with the motion picture occurred years later with his conversations with Sergei Eisenstein, the noted Russian motion picture director and theorist. Eisenstein had perfected the technique of montage, and what he interpreted as montage in Joyce delighted him.

In 1929 Eisenstein gave a series of lectures in London on film theory, in which he recommended *Ulysses* and Joyce's other works as advanced reading toward the development of what Eisenstein called filmic feeling.[3] The following year he visited Joyce in Paris. Joyce read and explained difficult passages in *Ulysses* to Eisenstein, who in turn told Joyce of his plans for a film portraying the course of thought through the mind. Eisenstein's theory was that only the film could do this job adequately. Before literature could do it, it must first break through the limits of tradition and orthodoxy. He singled out Bloom's monologues in *Ulysses* as literature's most brilliant achievement in this field.[4]

Joyce must have been somewhat impressed with this admirer, for he said later that if *Ulysses* were ever filmed, Eisenstein might be the man to do it. Apparently Eisenstein went so far as to write a rough shooting script of Bloom's internal monologues. Nothing came of this venture, however.[5]

The point here is that Eisenstein obviously had no

difficulty finding the visual aspect and sensing the visual possibilities of Joyce's writing.

Working by the light of Eisenstein's observations, Harry Levin entitles one of the chapters of his *James Joyce* "Montage." In this section he compares Bloom's mind to a motion picture, remarks that *Ulysses* has more in common with the cinema than with other fiction, and announces that Joyce's method of construction involves montage. Levin gives Joyce credit for understanding the technical possibilities of the cinema form, but reconciles this view with his later statement on Joyce's auditory imagination by maintaining that for Joyce the ineluctable modality of the visible was narrowed down, and that "blurred sight looked for compensation in augmented sound." [6]

Among others, then, Eisenstein and Levin have pointed out Joyce's keen interest in the motion picture form and his awareness of its potential. Of course, it does not follow that Joyce's writing was necessarily directly influenced by the motion picture form. It is true that Joyce at least had the opportunity to acquaint himself with this new medium in his formative period, and, as we shall see presently, there are techniques closely identified with the motion picture in his writings as early as some of the stories of *Dubliners*. But it would be patently impossible to prove that Joyce learned these techniques from the cinema. It seems more in order to suggest a parallelism.

One of the most remarked and familiar characteristics of twentieth-century literature is fragmentation. As Yeats says of our pluralistic world, "the centre will not hold," and what is left are pieces or fragments. This collapse of "public" truth is reflected in literature by the technique of fragmentation, in which the pieces or fragmentary images are held together, not by the cohesive power of commonly accepted traditions or standards, but by the synthetic and synthesizing power of artistic form.

176

We need not limit ourselves to Joyce in finding examples of this technique. T. S. Eliot, particularly in "Prufrock," "The Preludes," and *The Waste Land*, gives us a carefully controlled and significantly formed collection of fragments. This approach is found in most other twentieth-century poets and such prose writers as Conrad, Forster, Woolf, and Mansfield, to name only a few.

Fragmentary images fluidly combine, then, into a conceptual whole, under a rigidly controlled perspective. I suggest that this might be an exact definition of the motion picture form. Or we might say that the motion picture form represents an extension of the possibilities of this kind of literature. Because of the nature of the medium, the perspective in the motion picture is even more rigidly controlled. We look where the camera looks and nowhere else. And because of the motion involved, our continuing attention to what is being presented is necessary in order to grasp significance. In the motion picture we are not free to reread.

Granting differences inherent within each form, I think we can say that the two forms are essentially parallel. Starting from the common ground—the fragmentary perception of reality—these two analogous forms have evolved in our century, each employing controlled perspective, each using form as its synthesizing agent. The question then becomes, not, was Joyce's writing directly influenced by the motion picture, but, to what extent Joyce's writing parallels motion picture technique. Here the answer is clear. In his writings may be found parallels for every basic technique employed in the motion picture form, and in his approach to this form he goes considerably further than his contemporaries. His approximations of six standard motion picture techniques will be considered here: montage, superimposition, the overlap dissolve, flashback, controlled perspective or camera angle, and pictorial lighting.

The technique of montage affords a convenient starting point, because this technique has aroused the most comment by Joyce scholars. Indeed, this is perhaps the only motion picture technique that has been consistently ascribed to him. But to limit Joyce to montage is to oversimplify; although I use the term here for purposes of convenience, I shall presently differentiate Joyce's method from that of montage itself. To determine the nature of his deviation, it is first necessary to consider montage in some detail.

The technique was carried to its peak by Eisenstein in the 1920's. Discussing it at length in his book *Film Form,* he sees it as a succession of ordered fragmentary images. From this succession, or collision, as he describes it, arises a new image or meaning greater than, or different from, the separate images.[7]

The sources of Eisenstein's theory of montage are various. He speaks of certain experimental documentary films of the 'twenties, of his own experience on the stage, and of literary antecedents in Flaubert's use of "cross-montage of dialogues." More specifically, he credits three influences that at first glance seem totally unrelated: the Japanese Kabuki theater, Dickens, and D. W. Griffith. On closer examination, however, we see a logical genetic relationship among the three.

The Kabuki theater, according to Eisenstein, distinguishes itself in two areas. First, it has achieved the simultaneous and thus intensified presentation of aural and visual equivalents, the "monistic ensemble." Gesture, sound, and music all blend, thus reducing visual and aural perceptions to a "common denominator." Another characteristic of Kabuki which Eisenstein finds significant is what he considers to be its similarity to Japanese ideograph. He points out that each element of an ideograph corresponds to an object but that their combination corresponds to a concept. (For example, the separate symbols for "water" and "eye" combine to form "to weep.") This is the equivalent of montage in that the single "shots," each depictive, combine into intellectual contexts. He considers the Japanese poems known as *haiku* to be essentially ideographs transformed into phrases, and suggests that in literature Joyce has developed the depictive line of the Japanese ideograph.

In Dickens, Eisenstein points to the use of descriptive detail as foreshadowing montage. D. W. Griffith's contribution is clear: the close-up, on which much of montage depends. And Eisenstein appropriately points out Griffith's own acknowledgment of Dickens' influence in the development of the close-up.

To Eisenstein montage is the first and foremost principle of cinematography. In the structure of montage the individual shot is analogous to a cell, and it is the collision rather than the linkage of these individual cells which characterizes the structure. Eisenstein strongly dissociates himself from the concept of linkage, which he considers to produce "epic" montage, and adheres to the concept of collision, which he considers to be involved with "dramatic" montage. Since collision has dialectical connotations, his preference is not surprising.

Eisenstein views montage as similar in structure to emotive language, characterized by deranged syntax, compression, and logic of an affective kind. This is his point of entry to Joyce. In Bloom's interior monologues Eisenstein finds the most brilliant literary equivalent of montage. It is this aspect of Joyce's writing to which he confines his attention, and it is presumably the Eisenstein concept of montage which Harry Levin finds in Joyce. Levin also singles out the interior monologues as the central vehicles of montage.

But to take this view of Joyce's technique is to oversimplify. In the first place, Joyce follows the same general pattern of juxtaposed images and consequent intermittent pulsations both inside and outside the interior monologue. Second, he uses other visual techniques equally basic to his purpose. And finally, the Eisenstein concept of montage, although a fairly close approximation of Joyce's method, is not an exact equivalent of that method. There are important differences between the two.

In montage, the initial image tends to become lost, as does the frame of reference. If each shot or image is a cell in the structure of an emergent total and independent image, context, or concept, the initial point of reference becomes only the starting point, one of a succession of cells. But in Joyce this is not true. The starting point or image in most instances remains central. By an associative process other images cluster around this initial image or subsequent central images, but the initial image remains the controlling and persisting one. In interior monologue, this central image or frame of reference is the speaker of the monologue:

> His shadow lay over the rocks as he bent, ending. Why not endless till the farthest star? Darkly they are there behind this light, darkness shining in the brightness, delta of Cassiopeia, worlds. Me sits there with his augur's rod of ash, in borrowed sandals, by day beside a livid sea, unbeheld, in violent night walking beneath a reign of uncouth stars. I throw this ended shadow from me, manshape, ineluctable, call it back.

In this section of the monologue from the Proteus episode of *Ulysses* the central image—Stephen—persists and broods over the associated image clusters, containing them.

What prevents drawing an exact analogy between montage and Joyce's method is Eisenstein's term "collision of images." Although juxtaposition does of course imply collision, Eisenstein fails to take into account the pronounced interpenetration and persistence of images which we find in Joyce. A better word to use, I suggest, is "superimposition." This is what really happens in Joyce.

When we look for examples of superimposition of images in Joyce's writings, we suffer an embarrassment of riches. It will be helpful, however, to start with our primary concern, the *Portrait,* because in this work the technique has not reached the state of complexity or speed it achieved in *Ulysses* and *Finnegans Wake.* Although present in the *Portrait,* it is there in slow motion.

In its slowest form, Joyce's superimposition of images parallels the motion picture technique known as the overlap dissolve. In the straight dissolve, one image melts quickly into another. In the overlap dissolve, however, the second image is superimposed over the first, but the first image persists, gradually dying out. This technique is considered by theorists of the film to be a rhythmic device whereby one "note" is sustained before giving way to another.

It is quickly apparent that this is exactly what happens, visually, in many of the transitions Joyce makes from scene to scene in the *Portrait.* In each instance the final image of the previous scene persists into the following scene, flavoring and occasionally controlling it. This superimposition results in arrested or sustained notes. One of the first motifs in the *Portrait* is that of punishment. At the end of the very first section we are confronted with a poem about eagles pulling out eyes —a visual image with a vengeance. Juxtaposed to this is the next scene—a playground swarming with boys. But the poem lingers as if in prediction, and the image of the eagles dissolves slowly through the boys, who are the agents of conformity and thus of the authority that always seeks to punish Stephen—to pull out his eyes as it were. Thus Joyce, by "overlap dissolve," allows an image to die out slowly and, in the process, to govern what follows.

Another instance of this device is Stephen's dream about the dead Parnell. Juxtaposed to this is the Christmas dinner scene in which the violent argument about Parnell breaks out. In his dream Stephen sees a crowd of people at the water's edge watching an approaching ship. Word comes from the ship of the death of Parnell, but Stephen's Aunt Dante, disdaining mourning, walks proudly past the mourners. This dream image now dissolves into the following scene—the Christmas table—but broods over it, prophesying conflict. And Dante, of course, carries out her dream role by bitterly denouncing Parnell.

Let us consider, as another example, Stephen's louse:

> Yes, it was her body he smelt: a wild and languid smell: the tepid limbs over which his music had flowed desirously and the secret soft linen upon which her flesh distilled odour and a dew.
>
> A louse crawled over the nape of his neck and, putting his thumb and forefinger deftly beneath his loose collar, he caught it.

Here the "close-up" of the louse has been superimposed on the erotic reverie. The reverie dies out under the impact of this intruding image, which serves not only as an agent of deflation but as a semi-transparent filter through which we view the reverie in a new if squalid light. This superimposition induces Stephen's despair at his situation and leads to his ultimate renunciation of Emma, the object of his reverie: "Well then let her go and be damned to her!"

When the process of superimposition is speeded up, a new factor is added. Instead of one visual image gradually but completely dissolving into another, we have a central image that persists. Over this central image are superimposed subsidiary images that merge and dissolve into one another with varying degrees of rapidity.

The climactic episode of the *Portrait* offers a graphic example of this technique. In this scene on the beach Stephen, intermittently distracted by a group of bantering boys and the apparition of a hawklike man flying sunward, now sees a girl standing in the water and awakens to his true vocation: the artistic celebration of mortal beauty. Throughout this scene the central image is that of Stephen, and the superimposed images are those of the boys, the hawklike apparition, and the vision of the girl. These images blend and disappear, but the central image remains.

In the interior monologues of *Ulysses* the process, although greatly speeded up, is essentially the same. And it is here that the basic difference between Joyce's technique of superimposed images and the conventional view of montage can best be seen. In montage the image of the speaker—Stephen, Bloom, Molly—would be but one in a succession of images and would be lost in the next successive image, whereas in actuality the image of the speaker is the governing and containing image and is never lost. To refer again to the Proteus episode: "Ineluctable modality of the visible: at least that if no more, thought through my eyes. Signatures of all things I am here to read, seaspawn and seawrack, the nearing tide, that rusty boot." The orientation here and throughout the monologue remains unchanged. The fixed point of reference is Stephen's mind, upon the image of which are superimposed the various subsidiary visual images ("thought through *my* eyes"). Concepts of first person and the possessive help to differentiate this technique from montage.

Bloom's monologues are similarly oriented: "If little Rudy had lived. See him grow up. Hear his voice in the house. Walking beside Molly in an Eton suit. My son. Me in his eyes. Strange feeling it would be." In Molly's monologue the central image, the recumbent Molly, remains fixed.

"Superimposition," then, is a more accurate term to apply to Joyce's technique than is montage. The speed of the process varies greatly. In its slowest form it parallels the motion picture technique of the overlap dissolve. In its speeded-up form, as found in the interior monologues, it consists of a central persistent image upon which are superimposed a succession of disparate images, each displacing the one before and yielding in turn to the one after. The images in all instances are predominantly visual.

Visual superimposition is also present to a significant degree even in *Finnegans Wake,* described by Joyce as his "allnights newsyreel." This book, traditionally considered a composition primarily of sounds, achieves its visual dimension in the words themselves. In many instances word becomes image or, more accurately, a structure of superimposed images. Such word clusters as "abcedminded," "tabularasing," "indeedust," and "unbeurrable"—to name only a few—yield more to visual than to aural perception. As Joyce says in *Finnegans Wake,* "Our eyes demand their turn." The way in which our eyes receive their turn—that is, the way in which word as image works visually upon the reader-viewer—is best illustrated by one of the most significant portmanteau words in *Finnegans Wake:* "collideor-scape." This word cluster, itself a complex of superimposed visual images illuminating history and art, also illuminates the method and content of *Finnegans Wake.* Not only is the entire work a kaleidoscope of human history in which colliding fragments tend to assume different combinations as the focus of the scope is changed to provide escape from the collision, but each of the word clusters operates similarly. And the aspect of the imagination here called into play by both writer and reader is the visual.

Another form of superimposition is used by Joyce in his technique of flashback, also a component of film form. The technique of flashback is of course not limited to the motion picture—too many novels and poems testify otherwise. But motion picture flashback is a specialized kind, in which one visual image (of the past) is superimposed over another visual image (of the present) to begin the flashback sequence. It is this specialized form that Joyce frequently uses. As the young Stephen in the *Portrait* attempts to participate in a scrimmage on the playing field, the memory of a youthful conversation induces this kind of flashback:

Cantwell had answered:

—Go and fight your match. Give Cecil Thunder a belt. I'd like to see you. He'd give you a toe in the rump for yourself.

That was not a nice expression. His mother had told him not to speak with the rough boys in the hall. Nice mother! The first day in the hall of the castle when she had said goodbye she had put her veil double to her nose to kiss him: and her nose and eyes were red.

Later, memories of cold and repulsive wetness induce a visual flashback to the warmth of home: "How cold and slimy the water had been! Mother was sitting at the fire with Dante waiting for Brigid to bring in the tea. She had her feet on the fender and her jewelly slippers were hot and they had such a lovely warm smell."

These are but a few examples—there are many more. The important point to note here is that Joyce uses the kind of flashback peculiar to motion picture technique, in which one image is superimposed over the other. These images are usually visual; where there is a succession of images involved, the emphasis is frequently on the visual.

Superimposition is not the only visual technique of Joyce's which parallels the film form. He makes extensive use of the controlled perspective, which in motion picture terminology is known as camera angle. As was indicated earlier, the fragmentation prevalent in contemporary literature is one form of controlled perspective. Again, a specialized form of this technique is characteristic of the cinema. This is the kind of camera angle that takes in or includes a fragment of an object in the immediate foreground and shoots past it to the main content of the frame. For example, a shot may include a part of a mounted cannon in the foreground, but is directed primarily at a crowd milling in a public square. In this kind of controlled perspective or camera angle, the foreground is organically linked to the background. The fragment of cannon may suggest ominous possibilities or connotations of the milling crowd.

Joyce understood this specialized technique, and used it. In the *Portrait*, Stephen has an interview with the director of the school, who suggests the possibility of the priesthood to the youth:

> The director stood in the embrasure of the window, his back to the light, leaning an elbow on the brown crossblind, and, as he spoke and smiled, slowly dangling and looping the cord of the other blind, Stephen stood before him, following for a moment with his eyes the waning of the long summer daylight above the roofs or the slow deft movements of the priestly fingers.

The priest's hand, holding the noose, is in the foreground, and visually and significantly intervenes between Stephen and the world outside, thus controlling the scene.

In the Telemachus episode of *Ulysses*, Stephen, standing on top of the tower, is reminded of his dead mother:

> Stephen, an elbow rested on the jagged granite, leaned his palm against his brow and gazed at the fraying edge of his shiny black coatsleeve. Pain, that was not yet the pain of love, fretted his heart. Silently, in a dream she had come to him after her death, her wasted body within its loose brown graveclothes giving off an odour of wax and rosewood, her breath, that had bent upon him, mute, reproachful, a faint odour of wetted ashes.

Joyce, having established his point of reference in the foreground, now "shoots" past it:

> Across the threadbare cuffedge he saw the sea. . . . The ring of the bay and skyline held a dull green mass of liquid. A bowl of white china had stood beside her deathbed holding the green slug-

gish bile which she had torn up from her rotting
liver by fits of loud groaning vomiting.

The significant point here is Joyce's linkage of foreground to background, using as vehicle Stephen's
frayed "cuffedge." This image, epitomizing Stephen's
condition by suggesting the literal and spiritual poverty
of this motherless young man, is closest to our eye and
governs the scene visually. Dead mother is superimposed in flashback upon sea-mother, but the initial
point of reference remains fixed.

The final aspect of motion picture technique to be
considered here is that of lighting. It goes without saying that most authors reveal at least some sensitivity to
light and shadow in their writings. As in flashback and
controlled perspective, Joyce uses a specialized kind
of lighting in many instances, which is closely parallel
to that used in the film form. We may call it pictorial
lighting. Eisenstein regards this kind of lighting as a
collision between a stream of light and an obstacle.[8]
In several instances Joyce closely parallels this concept.
The source of light is invariably pinpointed, the light is
directional rather than diffused, and the "collision" of
the stream of light with various surfaces is depicted in
some detail. Several instances occur in *Dubliners*. The
young boy in "Araby" is talking to the girl with whom
he is infatuated:

> She held one of the spikes, bowing her head to-
> wards me. The light from the lamp opposite our
> door caught the white curve of her neck, lit up
> her hair that rested there and, falling, lit up the
> hand upon the railing. It fell over one side of her
> dress and caught the white border of a petticoat,
> just visible as she stood at ease.

A more remarkable example may be found in the opening of "Ivy Day in the Committee Room," which, in its
use of controlled perspective as well as pictorial lighting, reads like a screenplay:

> Old Jack raked the cinders together with a piece

of cardboard and spread them judiciously over the whitening dome of coals. When the dome was thinly covered his face lapsed into darkness but, as he set himself to fan the fire again, his crouching shadow ascended the opposite wall and his face slowly re-emerged into light. It was an old man's face, very bony and hairy. The moist blue eyes blinked at the fire and the moist mouth fell open at times, munching once or twice mechanically when it closed.

Similarly, examples are not lacking in the *Portrait:*

The chapel was flooded by the dull scarlet light that filtered through the lowered blinds; and through the fissure between the last blind and the sash a shaft of wan light entered like a spear and touched the embossed brasses of the candlesticks upon the altar that gleamed like the battle-worn mail armour of angels.

The use of this specialized lighting technique accentuates the sinister aspect of the priest who later interviews Stephen: "The priest's face was in total shadow, but the waning daylight from behind him touched the deeply grooved temples and the curves of the skull."

These various visual techniques are present in Joyce's writings not only independently but in combination. A representative section of the *Portrait*—that describing the Whitsuntide play in the chapel in Chapter II— offers a convenient example of this interplay. The perspective or "camera angle" is established at the outset as we see Stephen at the window of the dressing room watching the visitors arrive at the chapel. Pictorial lighting is employed: "under the sudden glow of a lantern he could recognize the smiling face of a priest." A series of carefully ordered fragmentary visual images establishes the scene in the chapel: barbells, Indian clubs, piles of gymnasium shoes, the vaulting horse. Stephen leaves the chapel, and again pictorial lighting sets the scene: "The light spread upwards from the glass roof making the theatre seem a festive ark, anchored among the hunks of houses. . . . A wide door of the theatre opened suddenly and a shaft of light flew across the grassplots." Stephen meets his comrades in the doorway, and "in the darkness, by the aid of the glowing cigarette tips, he could make out a pale dandyish face, over which a smile was travelling slowly, a tall overcoated figure and a hard hat."

Teased about his attachment to Emma, Stephen makes his mock confession. A flashback follows. The image of a previous inquisitional incident is superimposed over the present bandying. But the image of Stephen, motionless, contemplative, is the governing, containing, and static image.

The foregoing analyses make it apparent that Joyce's technique closely parallels in several ways that of the motion picture. I do not want to imply that Joyce "copied" film techniques. I suggest only that he was keenly aware of the possibilities of visual presentation, and used visual techniques extensively.

Nor do I wish to imply that the visual aspect of Joyce overrides the aural aspect—it does not. My intention has been to attempt to restore the balance that has been long absent because of the long-standing critical emphasis on sound and music in Joyce and the resulting picture of him as one who wrote primarily for the ear. His aural effects are well known and everywhere present in his works. He had a keen ear and he was demonstrably aware of musical effects and form. But clearly he was also at home in the visual, and achieved a considerable part of his most striking effects visually. And, as we have seen, the *Portrait* is not unique in this respect. What is true of it is true of the other works. Once again the *Portrait* serves as a guidebook for what is to follow and what has gone before.

Eisenstein speaks of "aural-visual counterpoint," which term may serve us here as a useful approximation of the total nature of Joyce's method. Joyce after all

189

is a communicator, and what he communicates is highly complex experience. By a complex and intricately organized contrapuntal pattern of visual and aural images, he endeavors to present the intermittently pulsative totality of experience itself. To a startling degree, he succeeds.

12

Joyce and Our Twentieth-Century World

THIS BOOK has examined some of the basic relationships that exist among Joyce's works and suggested a few of the meanings that the intelligent reader may perceive as he reads Joyce and thinks about him. But we have not yet confronted what may be a more basic problem —why *should* an intelligent reader spend a considerable amount of time reading Joyce and thinking about him?

Of course we may insist that Joyce is a major writer, a classic, but we must pin these terms down and look behind them. If we assume, for example, that Joyce is a twentieth-century classic, and press for specific reasons why this is true, we may discover several, depending upon our particular interest and approach. Students of literary history, for example, would of course be aware of Joyce as an experimentalist, an innovator. Analysts of literary influences would know that almost every important writer after Joyce was influenced by him, that the course of literature was changed by him in a way that may be said of very few writers.

But I suspect that, underlying these particularized reasons is the more basic perception of his supreme relevance to the world in which we live. This after all is the important issue; although Ben Jonson once said of Shakespeare, "He was not of an age but for all time," he had previously described him as the "soul of the age." In identifying a classic both of these descriptions must be taken together, because it seems clear that an artist must first be the soul of his own age—that is, must mirror his age and convey its essence, before he can transcend his age and stand "for all time." In other words, if a writer is not first relevant to his own age, he cannot very well be relevant to any other. The task at hand, then, is to establish Joyce's relevance to our twentieth-century world and give him at least that much claim on the future.

This problem of Joyce's relevance is multi-dimensional, partly because our world is multi-dimensional. The plain, often remarked, and not always happy fact is that we live in a complex, pluralistic, tentative world —a world that is unequivocally equivocal. How can we come to know this world?

Ultimately, of course, we cannot; however we approach it, we distort or oversimplify it. Science represents one imperfect attempt. It is a commonplace of twentieth-century physics that in attempting to measure things we sometimes distort them. One scientist says that it

> . . . is a little like asking questions of an exceedingly delicate and sick person through a crack in the door to his room in the hospital. You call in, "How are you?" He answers, "OK." But if he is very weak indeed the effort of making that answer may result in his death, so that the reply completely and automatically invalidates its own meaning.
>
> When a physicist asks an electron, "Where are you?" the electron replies; but the effort of replying always moves the electron—and unpredictably —into a new location so that the answer is automatically invalidated. . . . So the shocking fact is that science simply does not have detailed and

precise access to what we ordinarily call the external world.[1]

Our system of measurement may also distort by oversimplifying. An eminent physicist says that

. . . every measurement is an interrogation of nature and it is we who have arranged in advance a finite number of replies, while nature is always in the position of a voter in a ballot, with the difference that in the majority of cases nature is not given two balls, one black, one white, but a green and a yellow as well; indeed, the number may be 20, or even 10,000: but it is always a finite number. Nature never is in the position of a man filling in a voting paper on which he can write what he likes.[2]

If science, then, represents one of our imperfect attempts to approach and confront reality within a quantative frame of reference, literature is another imperfect attempt in a different frame of reference—that of human experience. Science and literature, moreover, share the same predicament—both of them oversimplify the reality they pursue. Literature might be defined as the esthetic organization of human experience; the very word "organization" shows that oversimplification has taken place. Obsessed by what the poet Wallace Stevens calls the "blessed rage for order," the writer superimposes order and pattern on experience, ordering and organizing it as he transmutes life into art and, in the process, distorts and oversimplifies. As Heraclitus pointed out some twenty-five hundred years ago, unity and order seem to reside in our minds rather than in our experiential world.

We are concerned here, however, with a particular kind of literature—symbolist literature—for it is this kind that Joyce gives us. Symbolist literature is less of an oversimplification of experiential reality than non-symbolist literature. As discussed in Chapter II, the symbol suggests many possible meanings rather than a single arbitrary one, and delineates an area of experience or a basic relationship. In this very inexactitude of the symbol we find a certain exactitude, a certain capability of dealing with qualitative terms—in other words, with the realm of human experience, with *value*. To put it another way, the symbol, because of its ambiguities, is the more capable of probing the ambiguities of experience in an uncertain, pluralistic world. The symbol's elastic, shifting boundaries permit it to assume the free-form configurations of experience itself rather than the strictures of conceptualized unity. It may be convenient to visualize a pebble dropped in a pool of water. Concentric circles expand until they reach the shore, where they take on the configurations of the shoreline. So it is in part with the literary symbol. The concentric circles are analogous to the multiple meanings radiated in the mind, and the irregular shoreline is analogous to the contours of experiential reality.

If I seem to belabor the relevance of the symbolist method to our world, it is because Joyce has always been under attack from one quarter or another because of his use of symbols as primary vehicles of meaning. Even today many still regard Joyce as artificially complicated. *Ulysses,* they say, is just a crossword puzzle, *Finnegans Wake* a guessing game. Currently there seems to be a discernible trend toward simple, straightforward narrative. But I suggest that if the pendulum has swung away from symbolism it will inevitably swing back again sooner or later, because it seems clear to me that this method, even with its admitted imperfections, is still the most honest way of confronting experiential reality through a work of art. If there is a better method, no one has as yet devised it.

It is not enough to find relevance in Joyce's method—we must find it in his substance as well. And I think we do. Joyce shows us what it is like to live in our world by giving us what we might describe as a multi-dimensional construct of that world. At the risk of over-simplifying, let us separate some of these dimensions.

There is, of course, that most obvious twentieth-century dimension, the psychological. As we have seen in *Ulysses*, Joyce, in his definitive use of the stream of consciousness technique, has probed and delineated the individual consciousness more deeply than any other modern writer. In presenting the seeming flux and disarray of mental processes, he reveals the spectra of the minds of the three principal characters of *Ulysses*—Stephen Dedalus, Leopold Bloom, and Molly Bloom—and in revealing them he reveals the nature of our own minds.

Another dimension of Joyce's construct or vision of our world is the ethico-moral. Joyce, although certainly not a moralizer, was just as certainly a moralist. Here, however, we must make an important qualification. Joyce believed, as have many of our major writers, that the work of art owes its primary allegiance to itself, that it must first maintain its integrity as art if it is to function as a valid and significant commentary on our world and ourselves. Joyce of course took his esthetic theory seriously, and he based and constructed it on the three principles of wholeness, harmony, and radiance that Stephen announces as the requisite qualities of the work of art in the *Portrait*. But his writings, owing primary allegiance as they do to esthetic integrity, do not operate in an esthetic vacuum. They concern themselves with our world and particularly with human values.

Further, on more than one occasion Joyce placed his writings in a moral frame of reference. In a letter to his publisher he said of *Dubliners:* "My intention was to write a chapter of the moral history of my country." At the end of the *Portrait* Stephen says: "Welcome, O life. I go to encounter for the millionth time the reality of experience and to forge in the smithy of my soul the uncreated conscience of my race." Joyce was never satisfied with only one meaning for a key term, and is seems likely that this "uncreated conscience" means in part "consciousness," particularly esthetic consciousness. However, conscience in its moral sense—that is, consciousness of the norms of human conduct—is obviously one of the things Stephen finds lacking in his fellow Dubliners, and the mission he announces for himself is partly that of creating an informing ethico-moral sensitivity in his countrymen. Perhaps it is at this point of sensitivity or awareness that the esthetic consciousness and the moral conscience begin to merge.

In presenting the city of Dublin to us, Joyce presents to us our world. To him Dublin was a microcosm; as Yeats said, "A great piece of literature is of its own locality yet translatable." Dublin, then, stands also for the world we know. One of the things Joyce shows us is a world of pervasive, omnipresent, stifling conformity. Dublin is a paralyzed city, strangling in the nets of conformity enforced by authority. This we know to be the pattern of Stephen's world in the *Portrait*. "Apologize, admit, conform"—these are the requirements of the social order in which he finds himself. These are the nets, and at the end of the *Portrait* he announces the means by which he will escape them: by silence, exile, and cunning. In "silence," we see his refusal to support the social order; in "exile," we see his refusal to participate in it or belong to it; and in "cunning," we see his determination to use any means—fair or foul—to circumvent, discomfit, or evade his enemies.

In *Ulysses* Stephen is still fighting the same battle against conformity, although now losing ground, and in *Finnegans Wake* also there is much about conformity. In the latter work Joyce seems to equate it with respectability in the eyes of the world. Shem, the so-called Penman, represents by and large the individual creative imagination, whereas Shaun the Post seems to stand for the noncreative or indeed anticreative group consciousness. Shem is a "farsoonerite," and would "far sooner muddle through the hash of lentils in Europe than meddle with Irrland's split little pea." In other words, he refuses to sell his birthright and chooses exile instead. And a part of this exile is ostracism— "All point in the shem direction as if to shun."

Clearly, from his earliest work to his latest, Joyce is centrally concerned with the polarity conformity versus nonconformity and with the plight of the individual who is caught in the web, struggling to free himself from the net of conformity reinforced by the harsh fibers of punishment or ostracism. This is a matter of peculiar and painful relevance to us. It is a problem we know about only too well in our twentieth-century world—in its ultimate ramifications it may be the major problem of the modern world. Joyce concentrates on the plight of the nonconforming artist, and yet the problem seems universal. The artist's is simply a test case—the acid test, the ultimate case. The maximum is at stake here. If conformity encases the artist, it smothers him and he dies. Quite probably this is Joyce's implication: that conformity enforced by authority smothers the artist in us all—the fresh, sensitive, individualized, creative aspect of our natures—that aspect so precious that to lose it is, in a certain sense, to die.

Joyce is not content merely to show us the young artist struggling against evil forces—he refuses to oversimplify that much. We must examine the other side of the coin also. And the other side is Stephen's arrogant, egocentric pride—his deadliest sin. Clearly he is at times a most irritating young man, with his intellectual and esthetic chips on his shoulder. He brandishes his creed in the face of both those who wish him harm and those who do not. In the end all men become his enemies. He dramatizes himself constantly, and often indulges in self-pity. He identifies himself with various martyrs: Parnell, St. Stephen, even Christ. Stephen's

197

ostracism and rejection by his contemporaries are at least partly self-induced. He is to some extent isolated by his own pride.

In a sense he is taking the easy way out by rejecting his world and running off to find another, rather than learning somehow to come to terms with the world in which he finds himself, and to bring beauty out of that world. The implication seems to be here that if he cannot learn these things in Dublin, he will not learn them in Paris either.

What Stephen desperately needs is a broad saving streak of humanity—a sense of kinship with his fellow man. His mother has put her finger on it. Her prayer for her son is that somewhere, somehow, he will learn what the heart is and what it feels. At times Stephen seems dimly aware of his need, but ironically he is oblivious to its real meaning—that he will never really achieve his announced vocation as a creative artist until he perceives and partakes of the common substance of man. He makes a religion of this esthetic, but overlooks the fact that he who would celebrate mortal beauty must first commune with mortality.

Shem, Stephen's projection in *Finnegans Wake*, is impaired for the same reason, and for this reason "Shem is a sham."

Joyce has given us, then, a double vision of society and the individual, of the public and the artist in our world today, and has indicated what is the basic need of each. Society, the group, the public—call it what you will—needs sensitivity, awareness, a respect for the individual creativity and difference, an acceptance of the nonconformist. On the other hand, the individual —the artist in this instance—needs the streak of humanity, the dose of humility that will purge him of his egocentric pride, to relate him to mankind. This, I suggest, is a penetrating vision of the plight of the modern world. As members of the social order we need to remind ourselves constantly of the sanctity of the individual. As individuals we need constantly the sense of responsibility and commitment to mankind. The lesson Stephen needs to learn is the lesson we all need to learn—how to be human, in the sense of humane. Joyce by implication anticipates the same question that Camus ultimately raises—how ought one to live?

This brings us to Leopold Bloom, the hero of *Ulysses*. Bloom is an amazing person, probably because he is so *un*amazing. It has been said that he is perhaps the best-realized "average" man in literature. As he walks the streets of the city on June 16, 1904, the day commemorated in the novel, we see the inside of his mind. It is a rather ordinary mind, by turns skeptical and gullible, sophisticated and naïve, filled with trivial information and misinformation, laced with a fairly standard assortment of decencies and indecencies.

How then does Joyce dare suggest that Bloom is a hero in any sense of the word, particularly within the heroic tradition? Bloom is, after all, supposed to be Ulysses. But some would be quick to say, what a falling off here—from glory to the inglorious! Is Bloom simply a parody of the Greek hero? Is Joyce simply stating that we have fallen on inglorious and unheroic times? Certainly many of the correspondences between Bloom and Homer's hero are comic in nature. The careful steering between Scylla and Charybdis in the Greek epic becomes Mr. Bloom stepping carefully between two arguing men on his way out of the Dublin library. The escape of the Greeks from the cannibals becomes Bloom throwing food to the seagulls.

Can we dismiss Bloom as a clown capering in the footsteps of an ancient hero? I think not. It seems to me that Bloom qualifies as a legitimate twentieth-century hero on more than one score. I say this in the face of such a book as *The Vanishing Hero* by Sean O'Faolain, whose central thesis is, as his title indicates, that the hero has all but disappeared from the novel of our time because there is no longer a universally accepted version of what constitutes the good life. In the place of the hero as a representative of the good life has come the anti-hero, who is constantly trying, not to define the norm, but to define himself—not to embody and transmit social sanctions, but to find his own sanction. This interesting thesis is ably argued by O'Faolain, but I would suggest that Bloom qualifies in part as a hero in that the hero is and always has been the embodiment of both the survival values and the norms of an age of culture, and that Bloom carries on this tradition in our own time.

For one thing, Bloom is amazingly resilient, and in our world resilience is patently of great survival value. Bloom is able to endure the buffetings of his environment, to weather the "thousand shocks that mortal flesh is heir to" in a way that Hamlet-Stephen is not. Bloom shifts, gives ground, strikes out in a new path. His father was a suicide, his only son died in infancy, his wife has taken a lover, he is persecuted on racial grounds. Bloom survives all this.

But there is more than mere survival or endurance here. In Bloom we see values or norms as well. He is essentially a man of kindness, of compassion. Many of his acts stem from feelings of humanitarianism. To be sure, these are minor acts and largely pass unnoticed. But the point is that Bloom undertakes these acts not out of any hope of personal gain but out of a sense of personal concern. At one point, for example, he helps a blind beggar across the street, and his interior monologue reveals his sincere compassion:

> He touched the thin elbow gently: then took the limp seeing hand to guide it forward.

> Say something to him. Better not do the condescending. They mistrust what you tell them. Pass a common remark.

Later, his compassion increases:

> Poor fellow! Quite a boy. Terrible. Really terrible. What dreams would he have, not seeing.

Life a dream for him. Where is the justice being
born that way.

Another of Bloom's central acts of humanity concerns
Stephen, driven to the wall by his past and present
failures and now drunk in a brothel. Bloom tries to
persuade him to leave, but Stephen is in a suicidal
mood and is eventually beaten by two equally drunken
soldiers. Bloom rescues him, brings him home with
him, serves him food, and thus in a sense offers him
communion with himself—with humanity. How complete this communion is is debatable—Stephen wanders
off into the night alone, afterward. But Bloom, acting
in simple compassion, has again offered himself and
his substance to another.

At one point in the novel Bloom states his beliefs
quite explicitly:

> Force, hatred, history, all that. That's not life for
> men and women, insult and hatred. And every-
> body knows that it's the very opposite of that that
> is really life.
> —What? says Alf.
> —Love, says Bloom. I mean the opposite of
> hatred.

Our final glimpse of him reveals another aspect of
his understanding—his acceptance of his world, his
fellow man, and himself. Isolated though he is, he
accepts life—accepts even the existence of his wife's
lover. And here is the final Homeric parallel, which is
a contrast as well. Whereas the Greek hero overcame
his wife's suitors with bow and arrow, Bloom has only
his equanimity. Yet this equanimity, this acceptance
or understanding or compassion—this weapon in our
time is at least as invincible as the bow and arrow of
the Greek epic. So it is we feel that Bloom will not
only endure, he will prevail.

Having presented us with his central characters and
what they have to suggest to us about human conduct,
Joyce compounds an already complex situation by his

use of irony. He takes great delight in poking fun at his principal characters and in deflating them. As we have seen, Stephen is rather frequently deflated—and so is Bloom. (Not so Molly, of course. She remains happily pneumatic to the very end.)

Joyce's irony is directed not only at Stephen, with his posturings, his arrogance, his greenness, but at Bloom as well. Bloom, with his eccentricities, erotic reveries, and stockpile of misinformation, is certainly at least partly a comic figure, and Joyce has fun with him. When Bloom leaves a restaurant immersed in a kind of gentle melancholy and self-pity, Joyce points to an inglorious analogy: "Under the sandwichbell lay on a bier of bread one last, one lonely, last sardine of summer. Bloom alone." Later, in a pub, Bloom is confronted by an Irish racist who makes increasingly pointed references to the fact that Bloom is a Jew. At first Bloom passes it off, but finally points out mildly that Christ was also a Jew. This enrages the citizen, and the scene becomes a farce. The citizen, upon hearing this mention of Christ, explodes and says: "By Jesus, says he, I'll brain that bloody jewman for using the holy name. By Jesus, I'll crucify him so I will." He grabs a biscuit box and takes after Bloom, who beats a speedy retreat out the door, jumps on a passing horse car, and gallops off around the corner with the citizen in hot pursuit. The comic dimension of the scene broadens as the horse car assumes the guise of a heavenly chariot: "And they beheld Him even Him, ben Bloom Elijah, amid clouds of angels ascend to the glory of the brightness at an angle of forty-five degrees over Donohoe's in Little Green Street like a shot off a shovel."

So Bloom is in part a ludicrous figure, trotting through a world that is at best grudgingly neutral to him and at worst openly hostile. The difficulty is that Bloom's plight here is in part our plight too. Parts of our world are clearly absurd, and our collision with absurdity, although often all too painful, has its comic aspects as well.

Let us remind ourselves of Joyce's helpful word "jocoserious." Joyce sees the world as a jocoserious world, in part absurd, in part meaningful. And man is jocoserious too—to be taken seriously in his aspirations, but to be laughed at in his pretenses and posturings. Joyce's irony is a way of reminding us that his affirmations are tentative. It is another dimension of his vision of reality. In its intermittent and pulsative qualities, it also possibly approximates the pulsative quality of our experience.

The final dimension of Joyce's vision that I should like to explore briefly is the metaphysical. When we speak of Joyce's metaphysics we are out on the frontier of Joyce scholarship, and I may say that it is rather lonely out here—not much has been done in this area.

The path that leads out here is a rather meandering one. On the opening page of the *Portrait* Stephen's father, who is described as having a hairy face and looking at Stephen through a glass, is clearly a child's idea and surrogate of God. In the course of the novel Stephen rejects this nominal father of his and casts about for a spiritual father. At the end of the novel he claims his mythical namesake, Dædalus the Greek artificer, as his spiritual father. But mythical wings are not strong enough to sustain Stephen on his flight into artistic freedom, and he falls.

In *Ulysses*, then, he has no father, and one important theme of the novel is of course the search for the father. Unmistakably, it seems to me, this is analogous to the search for ultimate reality, or for God, and it goes on all through the novel. The extent to which Bloom assumes the identity or function of Stephen's spiritual father is debatable, and it would seem that Stephen's search for ultimate reality will not be satisfied by an earthly counterpart.

— inventor, skillful craftsman

Stephen's attitude toward God fluctuates between defiance and terror. At one point in *Ulysses* he says that God is merely "a shout in the street," but throughout the novel he is tortured by the recurrence, in his interior monologue, of the Anglo-Saxon phrase, "agenbite of inwit." This again-bite of the inner wit or conscience usually associates itself with the apparition or memory of his dead mother, for whom he had refused to pray when she was on her deathbed. His mother also reminds him of Mother Church, whom he has rejected. And possibly even more important, it was his mother who had probed his main defect, an inadequate heart, an inability to love, which may in this context signify an inability to love God.

His uneasy relationship to God is reflected in his attitude toward the Church. He rejects the Catholic Church, but when one of his friends asks him if he intends to become a Protestant he retorts that he did not reject a logical absurdity only to embrace an illogical absurdity. The interesting thing, though, is that having rejected the Church, he cannot forget it. He goes out of his way to satirize its rituals. Clearly it is still a living thing with him, and he is not able to remain indifferent to it.

Another way of pursuing this path to the frontier is to view the *Portrait, Ulysses,* and *Finnegans Wake* in the large. If the *Portrait* is essentially the story of growth and flight, then *Ulysses* is the story of the Fall. It might be said that the three principal characters—Stephen, Bloom, and Molly—if taken together, stand as a sort of construct or analogy of modern man. If so, it is clear that there is one dimension of this modern man which is missing—the spiritual dimension. This may account in part for the loneliness, the isolation, the curious emptiness of their lives, and the search for meaning and reality that Stephen is involved in. Apparently human nature abhors a spiritual vacuum.

If *Ulysses* is the story of the Fall, resurrection is the

predominant theme in *Finnegans Wake*. There are resurrections on many levels, of which the title itself suggests one. Tim Finnegan's resurrection, brought about when whiskey is spilled on him at his own wake, seems, at first glance, a gross resurrection indeed. But Joyce took his etymology seriously, and the Irish word for whiskey is "usquebaugh"—"water of life." Thus there are symbolic overtones of baptism. Then too, Finnegan's legendary antecedent is Finn MacCool, the mythical slumbering Irish giant and folk hero, whose wakening (*Finnegans Wake* is Finn's again awake) suggests the resurrection of the heroic in mankind.

Resurrection in *Finnegans Wake*, however, involves much more than Finnegan and Finn MacCool—it involves us all. History is presented as cyclical, which in itself implies a certain kind of resurrection. We know of course that the Fall of man has been described in theological terms as *felix culpa*, the fortunate Fall— fortunate because it sets the stage for the redemption of man. In Joyce's pun in *Finnegans Wake* this becomes "foenix culprit." We as culprits have fallen, but as the phoenix, that mythical bird who rises from his own ashes, we are resurrected again.

So we arrive at the end of the charted area, and here a governing question confronts us. Is there implicit in Joyce's writings any concept of an ultimate reality— any notion of the nature of God? In other words, what is his metaphysics?

It is hardly necessary to point out that what I shall say about this is highly speculative, but it seems to me that the speculations are relevant ones. First, the world Joyce shows us is a world of polarities. Everything has its opposite or complement. Now to me, the concept of polarity itself logically implies a field within which the poles take position with respect to each other. Indeed, in the very process of recognizing the poles we inevitably postulate the field that contains them. This field may approximate Joyce's notion of ultimate reality or

God. And note the analogy that exists between this concept and the concept of esthetic form. Both are of the nature of fields or continua that hold in suspension, if not equilibrium, seemingly discordant elements. Stephen in the *Portrait* likens the literary artist to what he terms the "God of creation"; he thus emphasizes the analogy between the two. Is the implication, then, that the universe has been created as an artistic form? Has esthetics at this point moved toward metaphysics?

Let us reconsider the word "collideorscape" in *Finnegans Wake*—a word that seems to encompass much of Joyce's vision of ultimate reality. There are many possibilities of meaning here. Joyce may be setting up still another polarity—collision on the one hand, escape on the other. Collide or escape. Is this a commentary on history and art? Is it the dilemma we all face? To collide with life or experience and thus become enmeshed in it as Stephen feared he would be enmeshed in the nets? Or to escape into what? Exile? Or is there really this choice? Are we not instead, caught on the horns of the dilemma—to collide or to scape—and in this sense scape may mean to bear the guilt, as in scape goat. Is it the guilt of exile? Is the implication here that to escape is to avoid engagement, to abdicate, to bear guilt? These are perplexing questions, but through the welter emerges a different vision. "Collideorscape" is also kaleidoscope and the Greek roots of this word if translated literally, mean "to behold a beautiful form."

Finnegans Wake is itself in a sense a kaleidoscope. As we view it from different angles, it assumes different patterns. The patterns shift with the beholder's point of view. Pushing the analogy a step further, we may say that all literature is kaleidoscopic, that the patterns take and change shape with respect to the beholder.

There is a further implication. To refer back to Joyce's analogy between God and the artist, we sense that *Finnegans Wake* is an analogy of the universe, and what is more, of an ordered universe. When we behold it as an artistic whole we are placing ourselves, by the very act of beholding, on a higher plane—or in the continuum, if you will. We are outside the kaleidoscope, looking in, or looking on, and this presupposes a higher plane of existence from which the unity of the work is perceptible.

Experientially, then, we confirm the existence of this plane and we see that in contemplating the work of literature we are acting out on the human level the analogy of God contemplating the universe. The final question that seems implicit then is this: does the universe, as we know it, exist for the esthetic pleasure of God? If so—if this is the point toward which Joyce's implications tend—then *at* this point, esthetics and metaphysics become one.

As I have said, these are pure speculations, and need to be thought out a good deal more. However, they seem to open up new lines of inquiry into Joyce.

So, like *Finnegans Wake,* which is circular in form and ends where it begins, we come back at the end to where we began this chapter—with Joyce's relevance to the world we live in.

The world Joyce shows us in his writings is a strange world, chaotic at times. There is cruelty and there is compassion, side by side. Man's blundering and man's aspiration contend for man's destiny. It is a world in which man seems to have lost purpose at times, and yet a world in which he cannot tolerate being *without* purpose. Man is isolated—yet he searches for that which will end his isolation. And if his isolation persists, so does his search.

Yet underneath all this seeming flux is the hint, the sense, the recognition of form and order—the beautiful form of the kaleidoscope, perhaps—if we could but see it as God, perhaps, sees it. Yes, it is a strange world, an astonishing world, but it is a world we cannot help but recognize. For it seems to me that it is unmistakably *our* world, after all.

Notes

CHAPTER 1.

[1] For useful general accounts of Joyce see: Harry Levin, *James Joyce: A Critical Introduction* (London: Faber and Faber, 1944); William Y. Tindall, *James Joyce: His Way of Interpreting the Modern World* (New York: Charles Scribner's Sons, 1950); Marvin Magalaner and Richard M. Kain, *Joyce: The Man, the Work, the Reputation* (New York: New York University Press, 1956).

[2] See his Introduction to Joyce's *Chamber Music* (New York: Columbia University Press, 1954).

[3] See Magalaner and Kain, *op. cit.*, Chapter IV.

[4] Hugh Kenner, "The Portrait in Perspective," in *James Joyce: Two Decades of Criticism*, ed. Seon Givens (New York: Vanguard Press, 1948).

CHAPTER 5.

[1] Joyce dates the writing of the *Portrait* as 1904–1914. *Stephen Hero* seems to have been in progress from 1901 to 1906. Herbert Gorman, in his biography of Joyce, states that Joyce burned the *Stephen Hero* manuscript in 1908 and started the novel anew in a compressed form. Regardless of the exactness of these dates, it is clear that not much time elapsed between the abandoning of one version and the beginning of the other.

CHAPTER 6.

[1] See: Marvin Magalaner and Richard M. Kain, *Joyce: The Man, the Work, the Reputation* (New York: New York University Press, 1956); Hugh Kenner, *Dublin's Joyce* (Bloomington: Indiana University Press, 1956); William Powell Jones, *James Joyce and the Common Reader* (Norman: University of Oklahoma Press, 1955).

[2] See Richard Levin and Charles Shattuck, "First Flight to Ithaca," in *James Joyce: Two Decades of Criticism*, ed. Seon Givens (New York: Vanguard Press, 1948).

Chapter 7.

[1] See Richard M. Kain, *Fabulous Voyager* (Chicago: University of Chicago Press, 1947), p. 55.

[2] See William Y. Tindall's Notes to *Chamber Music*, p. 211.

[3] See: Melvin Friedman, *Stream of Consciousness: A Study in Literary Method* (New Haven: Yale University Press, 1955); Robert Humphrey, *Stream of Consciousness in the Modern Novel* (Berkeley and Los Angeles: University of California Press, 1954); Leon Edel, *The Psychological Novel* (New York: J. B. Lippincott, 1955).

Chapter 8.

[1] Louis Gillet, in his *Claybook for James Joyce* (London: Abelard-Schuman, 1958), reports that Joyce, commenting on the amount of time he had spent on the *Wake,* added: "Perhaps it is folly. One will be able to judge in a century" (p. 59). On another occasion Joyce is supposed to have ended an explanation of his method in *Finnegans Wake* with the question, "Am I mad?" (p. 91). Gillet also reports a wry comment of Joyce's: "Such a book, all in puns!" (p. 113).

[2] A useful summary of *Finnegans Wake,* together with a listing of characters which gives the reader access to the principal themes, may be found in Adaline Glasheen, *A Census of Finnegans Wake* (Evanston: Northwestern University Press, 1956).

Chapter 9.

[1] For an extended discussion of Joyce's esthetic doctrines, his borrowings and departures from St. Thomas Aquinas, see William T. Noon, S.J., *Joyce and Aquinas* (New Haven: Yale University Press, 1957). Relevant sections of Joyce's notebooks may be found in *The Critical Writings of James Joyce,* edited by Ellsworth Mason and Richard Ellmann (New York: Viking Press, 1959), pp. 141–148.

[2] In his Introduction to *Chamber Music,* p. 63, Tindall points out that the botanical name of cocoa is *theobroma* or "god food," and that "that probably explains Joyce's selection of that beverage as symbol" of the communion between Stephen and Bloom. Whether or not such communion does indeed take place seems highly problematical, however.

[3] Hugh Kenner, *Dublin's Joyce* (Bloomington: Indiana University Press, 1956), p. 126.

[4] T. S. Eliot, *The Complete Poems and Plays* (New York: Harcourt Brace, 1952), p. 196.

[5] C. G. Anderson, "The Sacrificial Butter," *Accent,* XII (Winter 1952), pp. 4–7.

[6] Kenner, *op. cit.,* p. 129.

[7] Irene Hendry, "Joyce's Epiphanies," in *James Joyce: Two Decades of Criticism,* ed. Seon Givens (New York: Vanguard Press, 1948), p. 40.

Chapter 10.

[1] Wyndham Lewis, *Time and Western Man* (New York: Harcourt Brace & Co., 1928), pp. 99, 100, 109.

[2] "The Portrait in Perspective," in *James Joyce: Two Decades of Criticism*, ed. Seon Givens (New York: Vanguard Press, 1948), pp. 154–155.

[3] William Y. Tindall, *James Joyce: His Way of Interpreting the Modern World* (New York: Charles Scribner's Sons, 1950), p. 17.

[4] In his Paris notebooks, written in 1902–1903, Joyce provides his answer to this interesting question. The cow would not qualify as a work of art because the man hacking at the wood did not have an esthetic end in mind.

[5] Eugene Jolas, "My Friend James Joyce," in *James Joyce: Two Decades of Criticism, op. cit.*, p. 8.

[6] Harry Levin, connecting the name of the Victorian melodrama from which Joyce got the "Penman" appellation for Shem, with the idea of Shem as a "self-searching" picture of Joyce, comments: "Jim the Penman is forging, with a vengeance, the uncreated conscience of his race." See his *James Joyce: A Critical Introduction* (London: Faber and Faber, 1944), p. 126. But Mr. Levin apparently does not connect this meaning of "forge" with Stephen's condition at the end of the *Portrait*.

Chapter 11.

[1] T. S. Eliot, "The Approach to James Joyce," *Listener*, XXX 14 October 1943, pp. 446–447; *The Portable James Joyce*, ed. Harry Levin (New York: The Viking Press, 1949), Introduction, p. 11; Richard M. Kain, *Fabulous Voyager* (Chicago: University of Chicago Press, 1947), p. 143.

[2] Herbert Gorman, *James Joyce* (New York: Farrar and Rinehart, 1939), pp. 86, 199, 201–202.

[3] Marie Seton, *Sergei M. Eisenstein* (New York: A. A. Wyn, 1952), p. 485.

[4] Sergei Eisenstein, *Film Form*, ed. and trans. Jay Leyda (New York: Harcourt Brace and Co., 1949), p. 104.

[5] Seton, *op. cit.*, pp. 149, 290.

[6] Harry Levin, *James Joyce: A Critical Introduction* (London: Faber and Faber, 1944), pp. 66–67.

[7] Eisenstein, *op. cit.*, p. 41.

[8] *Ibid.*, p. 40.

Chapter 12.

[1] Warren Weaver, "A Scientist Ponders Faith," *Saturday Review*, Vol. 42, January 3, 1959, p. 9.

[2] Erwin Schrödinger, *Science Theory and Man* (New York: Dover Publications, 1957), p. 73.